CULTURE AND HUMANITY IN THE NEW MILLENNIUM

Culture and Humanity in the New Millennium

The Future of Human Values

Edited by

Kwok Siu Tong and **Chan Sin-wai**

The Chinese University Press

Culture and Humanity in the New Millennium:
The Future of Human Values
Edited by Kwok Siu Tong and Chan Sin-wai

© **The Chinese University of Hong Kong**, 2002

ISBN 962–996–023–0

THE CHINESE UNIVERSITY PRESS
The Chinese University of Hong Kong
SHA TIN, N.T., HONG KONG
Fax: +852 2603 6692
      +852 2603 7355
E-mail: cup@cuhk.edu.hk
Web-site: www.chineseupress.com

Printed in Hong Kong

Contents

Introduction

Kwok Siu Tong and Chan Sin-wai

Despite technological advances, fluid borders and ease of communication, the world faces more challenges than ever before. Old values find themselves in new global contexts, locations have changed beyond recognition, and humanity has come face-to-face with issues that were barely imaginable a hundred years ago. What place will the Arts hold in the twenty-first century? There is an ancient Chinese term, *ren wen* 人文 which means "the art of humanity" and was one component of the three-fold Chinese universe that linked heaven, earth and humanity — the spiritual and philosophical, and the environmental and ecological. So according to this definition, the Arts are crucial to any discussion that impacts on culture, humanity and science.

Conscious of the rapid pace of change that has raised serious concerns in many fields, we invited some of the most celebrated figures in the international academic and arts community to come to Hong Kong and share their insights into the future direction of human civilization. This event, the International Congress on *Culture and Humanity in the New Millennium: The Future of Human Values*, which was jointly organized by the Faculty of Arts, The Chinese University of Hong Kong and the Home Affairs Bureau of the Government of the Hong Kong Special Administrative Region, took place on 8 January 2000.

A number of themes emerged over the three days of the Congress.

Firstly, and most basically, can universal values like love, togetherness, mutual aid, tolerance, which are advocated by Buddhist Master Hsing Yun in "The World in the Twenty-first Century," be accepted by the so-called humanities? Secondly, *are* there such things as universal values? Can we find values to prioritize worth as Laurence Thévenot in "Justifying Critical Differences: Which Concepts of Value are Sustainable in an Expanded Coordination" attempts to do? Does globalization mean an eventual unification within one outstanding value frame or can a plurality of representations sustain this process while maintaining critical differences?

Thirdly, can we accept pluralism over relativism as a guideline in developing a set of universal values? We can call these transcending guidelines for want of a better term. Are there such things as transcending guidelines for us to develop universal values? Professor Gerard Hughes argues in "Pluralism Without Relativism in Ethics" that moral pluralism, properly understood, accepts that there may be more than one acceptable moral code, while giving grounds for considering that difference between moral codes cannot be properly unlimited. Quite a number of Congress participants agreed with what he had to say.

The fourth point concerns the technological revolution. Technology, especially computers, does not always have positive effects as C. A. Bowers in "Cultural and Biological Consequences of Globalizing Computers," explains that computers, essential in most walks of life today, are not culturally or ideologically neutral. They reinforce the specific experience of the individual, giving them the authority to make moral judgments in isolation. They privilege print-based cultures, but negate the value of face-to-face communications. Paul Kan in "Creation of Wealth Using Knowledge Systems in the New Millennium" says that it is the knowledge and skill behind technology that has the real value. New ideas can be easily frustrated if society is not receptive to the chaos that may result from their introduction. We have increasingly recognized that there is a downside to technology, but what we need to do now is learn how to deal with it.

The fifth point is the claim that there is undeniable significance to the cultural components of music and literature. Violinist Isaac Stern in "The Central Importance of Music to Humanity in the New Millennium" shows us how music can join a disparate world together. He discusses its role in encouraging and developing the talents of the young, who will one day be the future leaders of the world. Wang Meng, a noted Chinese writer and literary critic, in "Who Is to Rescue Literature and Who Can Be Rescued by Literature?" sees Chinese literature as gaining new vitality in the new millennium, though it no longer acts as a "political weathervane." Both papers argue that there is something fundamental and undeniable about music and literature that we cannot ever totally ignore and that we do so at our peril.

Pauline Oliveros, composer, performer and founder of "Deep Listening," takes this a step further in her description of her theory of awareness in "Quantum Listening: From Practice to Theory (To Practise Practice)." Human values, she says, are developed through the experience of listening deeply to our surroundings, not just locally but globally.

The sixth point is, can cultural legacies be revitalized? Can cultural legacies gain new energy in regions like northeast Asia, as Shuichi Kato has argued in "Revitalization of Cultural Legacies in Northeast Asia?" This paper reinterprets some traditional philosophies in modern contexts, seeing these cultural legacies as assets that can be used to enhance moral values, aesthetics, and the work ethos. Using Hong Kong as an example, Ambrose King argues in "The Cultural Identity of Hong Kong in the New Millennium" that globalization does not have to mean cultural homogeneity nor loss of identity if a place is sure of its own culture values. Tu Wei-ming in "Confucianism in the Twenty-first Century: Dialogue Among Civilization and the Public Intellectual" insists that there is a place for Confucian humanism in the new millennium. Can cultural legacies provide guidelines in such rapidly changing times? Chou Wen-chung in "*Wen Ren* and Culture" holds the view that while heritage is the root of creativity, revitalization of that legacy calls for a response to stimuli from beyond that heritage so that it can adapt itself to the modern world.

The seventh point concerns local and regional knowledge. Can this kind of knowledge be developed into something universal? Is it possible that something area specific like Confucian humanism, be developed into a set of heuristic universal values open to all? Marc Ferro in "The Media and the Dispersion of Knowledge" discusses the tendency to separate knowledge into narrow boxes without the interconnectedness that usually applies. Our knowledge of history is also skewed by the concerns of the modern world which intrude on our depiction of the past. What we need is a more experimental way of looking at history, which may help us deal with the present and understand it better. Linda Nochlin, art historian and critic, talks on the over-hyped coming of the third millennium, and reminds us that perhaps not everyone views the celebration in quite the same way. Her thought-provoking talk on "Whose Millennium Is It Anyway? Beauty, Truth and Justice at the Fin-de-Siècle" concluded the Congress. She answers this question through a discussion of how the concepts of beauty, truth and justice are seen differently through the eyes of a number of modern women artists.

In conclusion, how can we make use of all these ideas, thoughts and suggestions? We have used a number of big words here, as demanded by our professions as academics, scholars, and artists. There are no ordinary people amongst us, no politicians and no powerbrokers of industry. Can we take our words and turn them into action? This is a question that will remain unsolved for a long time to come.

Acknowledgement

Our thanks are due to the Home Affairs Bureau of the Hong Kong SAR Government for co-organizing this Congress and to Professor Arthur K. C. Li, the Vice-Chancellor of The Chinese University of Hong Kong, for his support of this event. In the organization of the Congress, we have been helped by the generous sponsorships by a number of organizations, which include, in alphabetical order, the Asian Cultural Council, Air France, British Airways, China Airlines, Commercial Press (Hong Kong) Ltd., Consulate General of France, Hotel Furama, Japan Airlines, The Peninsula, Singapore Airlines, Tom Lee Music, and Ming Pao Newspapers Ltd.

In preparing the conference papers for publication, we are grateful to Ms Jennifer Eagleton for her translation of the article by Professor Ambrose King and her transcription of recordings of the speeches made by Mr Isaac Stern, Professor Tu Wei-ming, Professor Marc Ferro and Professor Shuichi Kato. We would also like to thank colleagues in the Department of Translation for their work in putting together this volume: Mrs Rosaline Li for her logistic support and Mr Bai Liping and Miss Eos Cheng Hui Tung for their transcription work.

The World in the Twenty-first Century

Master Hsing Yun

At the very beginning of the twenty-first century, it is a great honour to be invited by the Faculty of Arts of The Chinese University of Hong Kong and the Home Affairs Bureau of the Hong Kong SAR Government to come to Hong Kong and share with you my views on the theme of "Culture and Humanity in the New Millennium: The Future of Human Values."

Because of its highly volatile and unpredictable nature, the future is usually greeted with fear and uncertainty. With new technology and information overload, and the world changing at breakneck speed, there is even more fear of the future than before. The future that lies before us constantly changes our wisdom and adaptability, but it brings opportunity as well as crisis.

From time immemorial, people have turned to fortune-telling, sorcery, or the *Book of Changes* (*Yi Jing*) to reveal the future. But from the perspectives of history and Buddhism, the right approach is to vow to improve the well-being of our community, our society, our world and everybody in it, rather than waste time trying to discover what the future holds for us.

For example, the founder of Buddhism was a prince. After witnessing the sufferings of birth, aging, sickness, and death, the cruel victimization of the weak by the strong, and the injustice of the caste system, he was moved by compassion to exchange the luxuries of palace life for a long hard journey of monastic practice and cultivation. Ultimately, he realized the truth of the universe, notably the principle of Dependent Origination and the Buddha Nature in everyone. As he propagated the *Dharma*, during forty-five years of courageous striving to transform people's hearts and minds through education and cultural activities, he reshaped his destiny and the destiny of humanity.

Buddhism holds that everything, including human affairs, is subject to change, and is not predestined. Since the future is changeable, there are always opportunities for improvement. Telepathy and other extrasensory abilities used to be regarded as unachievable. But through the tireless efforts of scientists and inventors, we now observe at first hand events thousands of miles away, via television and the Internet. We communicate instantaneously with distant friends by radio and telephone. Ships and submarines, aircraft and spacecraft, carry us everywhere through seas and sky. By improving communication, we promote culture and advance mutual understanding and world peace. It is true that we cannot predict the future, but our destiny in fact lies in our own hands. We must limit our possibilities.

What does the words of the twenty-first century look like? I would like to share with you six points, and hear your comments.

The Twenty-first Century from the Perspective of Politics

In earliest times, political power was concentrated in a single person, usually an emperor. After numerous revolutions, political power gradually devolved to the people. When they found that their collective rights were generally inadequate, attention shifted to issues of individual rights. Concern for basic rights focused on one person. At the same time, people came to realize the importance of their surroundings, and tried to defend wild animals in their habitats and protect forests and other lands from the ravages of development. Henceforth, ecological balance was a major public issue, and played a major role in the policy deliberations of national leaders and at international summit meetings. Out of concern for biodiversity and ecological balance, issues related to living rights have now gained the attention of mankind. The advance in bio-technology and genetic engineering has contributed much to eugenics, genetics, and pathology, but it has aroused as many concerns and provoked debate on the meaning of life and morality. The legality and morality of abortion and euthanasia are also issues of current concern. In my view, living rights will be an important issue in the twenty-first century.

The Twenty-first Century from the Perspective of Religion

Fear of the unknown led primitive people to attribute natural phenomena like thunder, lightening and storms to divine acts. Even today, when people attribute global weather changes to "El Nino," they are referring to the "Holy Baby," i.e. Jesus Christ. In archaic animistic religions, people attributed such natural occurrences as birth, aging, sickness, and death to the actions of spirits, ghosts, and gods. They believed that these beings were all around them. In a later development, deceased heroes were glorified and deified. Temples were erected for their worship, because they were thought to protect their devotees. In our scientific age, such beliefs are no longer acceptable. Armed with greater knowledge, people realize that there are causes and conditions of all phenomena. From now on, the religion that explains the Principle of Dependent Origination and the law of causality will grow increasingly popular. The religion that respects the truth will survive the test of time. It will guide people and give real peace of mind, not mere talk. Its liturgy will inspire its adherents. It will be relevant to daily life, not a heresy or superstition. Its founder should be a real person of high morality and pure behaviour, not a fictional character. It will guide people towards wholesome goals that benefit society, not to mundane material gain. Under the guidance of the religion of truth, people will open their minds, and increase their fortune and wisdom daily. Then the world will be full of brightness and joy.

The Twenty-first Century from the Perspective of Society

Human societies undergo gradual evolution. China, for example, evolved from a nomadic into familial one. As the population grew, tribes emerged and tribal societies took shape. In time, nationalism emerged among neighbouring regions that shared a common language, customs, traditions, and blood relations. The nineteenth century unleashed the power of nationalism, as many captives rallied to free themselves from colonial status. In the twentieth century, warfare still smoldered and human suffering continued unabated. People began to realize that peaceful coexistence of nations required mutual respect and assistance. Only through negotiation and communication would "win-win" situations be possible. In the last decade, we witnessed the fall of the Berlin Wall, the creation of the European Union, the increased communication and cultural exchanges between mainland China and Taiwan, the peaceful handover of power in South Africa, and the formation of the North America Free Trade Area, Asia Pacific Economic Cooperation, and the World Trade Organization. All of these pave the way for a world in which all of us "coexist" compatibly. We have made much progress; let us appreciate and value these achievements, and work even harder for a twenty-first century of joy and harmony.

The Twenty-first Century from the Perspective of Economics

Economic activities are among the most important aspects of human life, for they involve fulfilling the most basic needs. Spiritual needs and human dignity are achievable only after basic economic needs are satisfied. Human beings began their economic life by hunting, fishing or cattle herding. After a long period, agricultural economies emerged when nomadic peoples settled down and cleared land for planting. In later ages, the invention of complex machines led to the emergence of the industrial economy. Cars, telephones, air conditioners, refrigerators, washing machines, heaters, etc., became part and parcel of our everyday lives. Television, audio and video recorders, the high tech industrial products, added colour and variety to our homes and lives. The rapid development of computer science and Internet services significantly transformed our traditional lifestyles, and while financial, medical and recreational services became readily accessible. We have now entered an economy of information technology. At the present rate of technological advance, it may soon be possible to invent computers that are human-like, able to differentiate and react to colour, sound, smell, taste and touch, and exhibit patterns of thought. In the "mind economy," we can use the power of our mind to work wonders. A world in which the mind governs our surroundings, as described in Buddhist sutras, may soon be a reality! We can foresee that our world in the twenty-first century will be colourful, wonderful and interesting.

The Twenty-first Century from the Perspective of Life

People used to work daily to satisfy their basic need for food and clothing. This is the so-called "material life." Beyond basic needs, however, people began to pursue a life of the spirit, including education and religion. Next came the arts. Professional artists, pianists, singers, and dancers emerged in large numbers, especially in the second half of the twentieth century, in the developed countries. The arts became an important part of people's lives. Both workplace and home were embellished with art objects and antiques. Having gone through stages of material, mental, and artistic lives, people in the twenty-first century will find that these may not satisfy their needs and expectations. They will again pursue a religious life that balances the material and the spiritual. Such a balanced life is called the "middle way," and it leads to peace and harmony.

The Twenty-first Century from the Perspective of Education

Education is the cornerstone of progress and development. In the most rudimentary education system, a tutor was employed to coach several pupils. As the number of students increased, classroom education became necessary. To provide continuing education, however, educational broadcasting was developed, relying on radio and television. In some developed countries, all existing educational facilities are unified through computer and Internet services, enabling students to learn quicker and more effectively, and providing interaction between the teacher and the students. Geographical and other physical barriers are thus overcome, and students thousands of miles apart communicate with each other. Virtual reality has added a new dimension to learning. For example, we can now follow by computer the performance and outcome of distant experiments. Scientists are working on an even more ambitious project: exploring communication through thought patterns.

Such developments have generated vast improvements. Above all, they may even help us realize the Truth of Oneness. This will certainly be a trend in education in the twenty-first century.

Conclusion

As I have said at the beginning of this article, there are six major dimensions that we should examine at this turn of the century. These cover the perspectives of politics, religion, society, economics, life, and education. The twenty-first century will be a better and happier Pure Land if we pay attention to living rights, propagate a religion of truth, strive for a coexisting society, work towards a "mind economy," follow the middle way of life, and realize the "Truth of Oneness." Let us work together to reach our goals.

The Central Importance of Music to Humanity in the New Millennium

Video Address by Isaac Stern

Good morning, good afternoon, good evening — whenever this may be where you are.

Ladies and gentlemen, or should I be up to the moment and say ladies and gentlemen dotcom, as everything else today seems to be dotcom. And maybe that is part of the problem of the discussion you will be having about cultural values in the new millennium and their effect on the human conditions, which I think is the basis of this meeting.

I can only speak from personal knowledge about music and what music education can do for the minds of young people. But, in effect, it will have to do with almost every subject that you, my colleagues, whom I regret not being with today, will discuss.

You will be discussing each in your own disciplines or perhaps in the cross-disciplinary discussion just how can humanism/humanity play a more important role in the development of nations large and small, and what are their individual responsibilities, these nations to each other, and how can they take advantage — true advantage — of the greatest single wealth that the whole of this earth has: the minds of its young people. That I think is the challenge that each of us in our own disciplines faces and what we have to try to show by deed, and by thought and by care, how much we can bring to young minds a view of humanity as a whole, the idea that to ask questions is to learn, that to be curious at all times throughout your life is the most important thing a human being can be, and to give, to some degree, an understanding, which is the beginning of respect, an understanding of what different values, cultural values, societal values are in different countries, and how they can be respected and yet be a part of the whole.

Obviously I do not agree or nor will I ever agree that homogeneity — being the same — is either necessary, good or at all interesting. It is the very difference between peoples and cultures, the way young people grow and how they learn to take up the responsibilities of the nations in which they live that should be embraced. I think that in smaller countries, it is an even more difficult task because democracy is a word, not a fact the world around. Whether democracy is established because other countries like the word or the way it operates — can indeed operate — in the growing pains of the changes of a society is a question I am not equipped to answer. But democracy essentially means more than just the right to shout against your government or the possibility to have a loaf of bread, or to wear a pair of jeans or to listen to pop music. That is not democracy, although that passes for democracy in many countries.

The idea of individual responsibility in a society is something else. And only democracy, democratic societies make it possible for young people to join together politically because they care, and because they know, and because they have been given the right to ask questions and question authority, only then can the democratic principle really come into focus.

What does all this have to do with music? I'm supposed to speak to you about what I believe and this is part of what I have been saying to youth until now. I have been involved with young talents for over forty years. In the last eight or ten years, it has become more organized so that I now call them "encounters" — chamber music, in Jerusalem, in New York, in Holland, in Germany, in Japan, in China and now to other countries as we are discussing at this moment.

You will note that I use the word "encounters" — they can be any-where from a week to three weeks — I do not call them master classes. I believe sometimes in the purity of words.

Master class for me means that someone comes in, and takes a young talent and breaks down all the bad habits and all the difficulties that have caused problems. But having done that, you will have to be there to put the pieces back and that is not done overnight. That may take three months, six months, certainly not a question of days or a few weeks. Three weeks is a wrong, wrong period — it is too short.

I have neither time nor the patience for that kind of long-term relation-ship with a group of students. What I am interested in is to get into the minds of the young people who play for me. I do not bring my violin because I do not want them to copy. I want them to think. I want them to learn how to feel what they are doing, how to realize that music is not those little black dots on some paper with lines, but how do you get from one dot to another, that millisecond between notes, which is where music begins.

And when young people begin to feel to understand the power of that language, and you can show them a few physical facts about what is effective bow speed, vibrato, all the technical things that go into playing a string instrument — they suddenly discover they have their own voice, not yours, theirs, and that is important. They start to think. You have to teach them how to read to understand that there is a whole life, a cultural history behind every creative beauty that man possesses, whether in music, painting, dance, sculpture, ideas.

Behind every creative genius — that is a word I use rarely because a creative mind to me is a genius — we as performing artists are recreative. I do not use the word "genius," I use the word "talent." For me, genius means creativity. Behind every creative spirit there was something in the background — the education, the people, the way the country lived, what we call totally, a culture. And out of that culture came a voice that recognized possibilities, and in some cases truths about the human condition within that spirit, whether it be Mozart or Shakespeare or Da Vinci or Diaghilev… everyone in their own language recognizes what was possible in the life of human beings living together.

Now I believe that young children — when I say "young," I mean from pre-kindergarten through the eighth grade — that they are the ultimate responsibility of the society, that is all of us, no matter in which society we live. I believe in getting to those minds, at the very beginning, to teach them how natural it is to see beauty, to teach them the range of sounds and colour in music or painting or in movement in dance, to teach them how each of them can become a person in their own way. This is what our responsibility is within each of our cultures.

Children are not born to hate; someone has to teach them that miserable act. They are competitive but they don't hate. It takes a very mean society or fault in the home, in the whole school or in religion that teaches them to think of other children as "they," "us" or "them."

Music perhaps more than any of the other arts is the most natural for children. Why? I use this example many times. Because when the fetus is still in the womb, the heart is beating as the first pulse, the first tempo. The moment a child is born "ah…" — pulse and sound — the basis of music. Children recognize that instinctively. They react to it instinctively. And they recognize its validity to their being a person instinctively. What I am trying to say is all these matters can touch on the way, a city, a town, a village can live. Then a state, perhaps a country.

I have rose-coloured glasses as far as humanity is concerned. I believe that everything can be possible if there is a passion for making things better, not only in one way, but better in many ways. I believe that through the interactivity of young people of all backgrounds, of all colours, of all religions, they learn to recognize each other as friends and they can create a different society.

I think that possibly if I had the opportunity to wish for one thing in the world more than anything else, I would wish that in every country, regardless of its present political or economic state, that every country would learn that to be a teacher — a qualified teacher, an informed teacher, a caring teacher, who knows how to get into the minds of the students, should be the most highly honoured, the most highly paid member of society, because into the hands of the teachers, we give the future.

If we do not recognize our responsibilities to make the art of teaching, the greatest single, international profession, we may be doing ourselves more harm than all the good arising from the discussions taking place during this Congress. I think that teaching is the only way that respect for other peoples' ways, other cultures, other ideas, and other habits can be obtained. It has to be obtained also with the knowledge of what cultures are and also recognize what the weaknesses of culture have been. The history of man, internationally, is not great. Wars have been common phenomena, and the growth of religions — who say "only ours is the one true religion" is increasingly common. For young people, it is the unknown which is the most fearful. But with knowledge, there is no reason for anything to remain unknown.

As a musician, I know what participation in music can mean to young people and how it can bring them together. As fellow musicians, they don't look at colour, they don't look at gender, they don't look at the area or the culture from which their friends come, they learn to accept because that is the way the friend lives, a friend that one loves.

I don't know where this discussion will go. I am sorry that I cannot be with you and be a part of the discussion. I only wish it were possible because it is the way I like to do these kinds of informal meetings. I am not a speaker in the official sense, and I never write a script. I have to speak as I feel at the moment. But normally I say a few words of generalities along the lines I've been discussing even when I ask for questions from the audience. With such a distinguished group I would have looked forward to hearing your questions and seeing to what degree we could cross each others' lines of communication to see where we come together and where we digress.

It is my understanding from the outlines that I have been given that this is a meeting to find out how to begin to understand and work together, and I shall be curious to read how each of you answer that question and to what degree each of your disciplines will touch on the various facets. I think I can say safely, finite answers cannot come out of one meeting. Ideas can come out, the possibility of certain kinds of experimental education can come out, and a mutual belief in the validity and the importance of fine minds can also come out which can be passed along to teachers and teachers to students. Teaching, education, humanity, the willingness to believe in something one thinks as beautiful, and to respect somebody else's ideas will emerge as well. It's a tall task.

The history of the second half of the twentieth century is a very mixed one. It saw some of the darkest moments of inhumanity, of bestial use of political power, of horrible acts done against people because they were "different." At the same time we have seen the most enormous increase in medicine, in science, in communications, in the speed of travel and the disappearance of any place on earth that can't be seen by the rest of the world almost instantly.

It is a new world that all of us have to learn to live with. It is a new world of technology that we must become masters of, not slaves to. There is so much that can be done. People can do things with eyes, with blood, with hands, with limbs, with anything today in medicine that were not dreamed of fifty, sixty, seventy years ago. The growth in biochemistry in the last thirty, forty years is enormous. The very changes that have taken place have gone at a faster rate than perhaps any other century that man has known since we have begun to learn to count time.

To take any of this out of context just to focus on just one small thing is perhaps an easy way but it won't be the true way, in the same way that people have to learn to respect different cultures. We have to respect the instruments that we are being given that are faster than anything we've ever had to use. Along with the instantaneousness of being everywhere and the speed of travel has come the speed of destruction. It was not thus fifty years ago. It took more time, and when there was time, there was time perhaps to think. Now things can happen quicker than one thinks. A few madmen, a few insane zealots, can change the course of political and cultural history in the space of hours.

So for those of us who are here, I, in this slightly disembodied way, regretfully greet you, my colleagues, and the organizers who have gone to such careful lengths to have this meeting occur, and have everything arranged to the ultimate satisfaction and comfort of the participants. I wish you all a most healthy, happy, and accomplished year in the year 2000, and I will come back to one thing. We are responsible for the minds of the future. Nothing else is more important.

Wen Ren *and Culture*

Chou Wen-chung

Half a century ago, as I was searching for a way to merge the modern West and ancient China in my music, I was overwhelmed by these poetic lines of Chen Zi'ang 陳子昂, who lived at a time when the Chinese culture had just emerged out of the chaos:

前不見古人
後不見來者
念天地之悠悠
獨愴然而涕下

I see no one before me,
I see no one after me;
All alone, overwhelmed by the thought of
    the eternity of heaven and earth,
My tears fall.

In the 1950s there was hardly a flicker of creativity in Asia. Chinese culture was in a void. Today all of Asia is again alive with creativity. A myriad of gifted artists as well as scholars and scientists are making contributions not only in Asia but also in the West. Unfortunately their contributions are made individually and without a cultural context, while their own societies appear to remain suspended in a void, as they have been for centuries. The apprehension that I shared with this poet of one and a half millennia ago remains as disturbing today as ever. While there is evidence that the Asian world remains rich with exceptional men and women as in ancient times, serious questions must be raised as to which society their works contribute to, or is it to the world, and what their roots are, or whether roots are superfluous today. Answers to these questions raise doubt whether we are indeed at the dawn of a new era in Asia.

I am not a historian or philosopher, nor an anthropologist or sociologist. I was born in the first quarter of the last century; and what has happened to Asian culture since then has been a matter of grave concern to me. I can only speculate on the developments of the century on the basis of personal observations and reflections, as well as personal involvement and creative experience over the decades. I am a composer, and my roots are of the Han culture of China. But I believe all artists of our time must have awareness and commitment that cross disciplinary and cultural boundaries.

I was born in an age of turmoil, between the 1911 Revolution and the 1927 campaign against the warlords. My childhood memories consist mostly of running for safety. My awakening to my Chinese heritage took place in the harsh environment of savagery and devastation during the eight long years of Japanese invasion in the 1930s and 1940s. For me, suffering leads to faith and faith leads to the search for roots. I began to research Chinese culture as well as music, shortly after my arrival in the United States in 1946, when I was challenged by Nicolas Slonimsky, the legendary musicologist-conductor-composer, as to what heritage or heritages my music emanated from. So in the 1950s I began a lengthy period of studying the music of Asia, after I was required at Columbia University to pursue advanced studies in the early history and theory of European music. I did so, because I asked myself why should I exclude my own heritage from my development as a composer?

By the middle of the 1960s, I became involved in musical activities in Asia. I urged Asian composers and scholars to launch an international organization of their own to foster the development of music in Asia. I was concerned as to why and whether Asians had to rely on American or European learned institutions for the development of their own cultures. I still remember vividly how this conversation took place with José Maceda, Lucretia Kasilag, and Hsu Tsang-houei, among others, at a garden reception in Manila for the International Music Symposium of 1966. After another meeting in 1977, a large gathering of leading artists in Beijing, including Wu Zuoren and Yang Yinliu, I established the Center for United States-China Arts Exchange at Columbia University, to encourage the long isolated artists, scholars and educators in China to interact internationally, and to promote understanding of Chinese culture in the United States. For ten years, we at the Center actively carried out exchange projects in arts disciplines ranging from architecture to theatre. The 1983 production in Beijing of *Death of a Salesman*, directed by Arthur Miller himself, inspired more than 150 new experimental plays by young Chinese playwrights within a year, as Cao Yu told me. We carried out an ongoing project on arts education which, after eight years, motivated the Chinese government to establish a ministerial level of sub-commission on arts education.

In 1990, in collaboration with Leonard Bernstein and the London Symphony Orchestra, the Center enlisted more than a hundred young musicians from the Pacific regions for the first Pacific Music Festival, held in Sapporo, Japan. Concurrently the Center had organized the Pacific Composers Conference with about fifty composers ranging in age from early twenties to the late seventies, the oldest being Isang Yun, to examine the role for and the roots of the Pacific composer.

Since then, the Center has been dedicated to the conservancy and the development of the twenty-five indigenous cultures in Yunnan, China. The idea is not to limit our efforts to these cultures alone, but to learn about issues facing all cultures. With this in mind, we enlisted the active participation of many Southeast Asian experts in our tasks in Yunnan for the past ten years. Concurrently we also conducted a multi-year study of conservation and development of the built environment in ancient cities with historic cultural legacies, such as Yangzhou. In September 1999, as the Center's last project for the twentieth century, we organized the International Leadership Conference on Conservancy and Development, with almost a hundred participants from abroad and even more from Yunnan and China at large, to consider how culture, ecology, economy and society can best interact with each other in communities around the world, especially those facing disintegration and extinction in the face of economic development and modernization.

These involvements in Asia are intertwined with my activities in the United States as composer, researcher, educator and arts administrator. Equally important to me, during all these decades, is my involvement in another direction. My continuing commitment to studying, editing and completing the compositions of Edgard Varèse, my mentor, keeps me in contact with his roots — those of Europe. He was profoundly knowledgeable in traditional European music and, as a young man, was deeply impressed by the innovative ideas of his mentors, Debussy, Busoni and Strauss. However, he was determinedly independent of the past and the present, in order to reach out to the future — a future illuminated by his own music and ideas. Reviled and all but ignored during his lifetime, he is now a source of inspiration for young Europeans. Another composer I learned a great deal from, though not personally, was Bela Bartok. What he taught is the metamorphosis of seemingly simple folkloric ideas from his native East European culture into a sophisticated modern grammar for music which in turn made a long-lasting impact on contemporary musical language. His greatest lesson is in his admonition that in studying non-Western music, one must consider the character and tradition of its culture as well as all the inherent qualities of the material itself, not all of which are perceptible or definable according to Western concepts. This is a great principle that few Asian artists have paid attention to.

Fifty years of learning, questioning, experiencing and deliberating have convinced me that if one admires the achievements of Asia in the past and believes in the future of its cultures, one must be as severe a critic of its present, as history has been of its past. Only then is there a future to hope for. Being critical alone is not enough. One must be actively engaged. Only then is there a future. To learn about the future, we must understand the present. To understand the present, we must know the past. For me the present is the past half-century, and the past is the millennia before then.

Let us look at the 1950s, the decade immediately following World War II. In the West it was a time of restoring normality, of returning to cultural and other peaceful activities. It was also a time for solidifying and integrating European cultures after years of chaotic relocation of artists and their works throughout the Western world. As it happened, it was a time of conclusion for the artistic aspirations begun in the waning decades of the nineteenth century. Simultaneously, it was also a time for awakening to new stimuli: exploration of scientific and technological advances, and exposure to the artistic legacies of other cultures — mainly Asian. Chronologically, it also happened to be a time of maturity for the older generation of artists, who were the architects of modern Western culture, and a time of emergence for the younger generation, their rebellious successors. These two generations together have since defined not only twentieth century Western culture, but in reality the culture of the world.

Meanwhile, in the East, it was a time of continued chaos and destruction after the war, a time of groping for survival after centuries of colonialism. It was a time of ongoing economic and ideological struggle. It was not a time for valuing one's own legacies or nurturing artistic explorations for the future. Innovation in the arts and education in culture were regarded as luxuries or frivolities that Asian societies could not afford or would not engage in. If there were art and culture, it was imitation — the ugly manifestation of a colonial psychology that finds security in worshipping past occupying powers. Thus, Asia was then, as before the war, filled with the work of emulation of European and Soviet art of another time. Economically and politically, the struggle in the 1950s did eventually lead to a brighter economic future. Culturally, however, neglect in the arts and education led to a void, contributing to further erosion of heritage and massive collective loss of memory.

Happily there were exceptions — even if only a handful. Surprisingly, there were Asian artists who had, solely on their own, nourished their roots and experimented at transcending cultures, without copying the modern West, or echoing the Asian past. It is to those few that all Asia should be thankful. Their dedication may eventually re-ignite the creative spark that continues the great cultures of Asia.

Presently, increasing waves of aspiring young Asian artists have become exposed to fast-moving Western artistic developments. Inevitably, however, for lack of living legacies of their own, they have also become dominated by Western trends and fashions. Few are able to assert their own heritage, stand firm independently, or transcend cultures. Nonetheless many of them have become influential in their own societies. During these decades, some societies have also demonstrated impressive growth in cultural activity. But such activity as a rule has not demonstrated relationship to the society's own heritage or legacies.

To make things worse, recent decades, which coincided with China's rapprochement with the West, witnessed a steady erosion of the arts in the West. The following phenomena have taken place: the passing away of so many great creative artists of the century, the rise in awareness of non-Western concepts and practices, the historic social change in Western societies, especially in the United States, the all-pervasive commercialization of every aspect of society, including health and the arts, the most personal needs of humanity. In the arts, this has led to the inevitable loss of distinction between creative expression and commercial enterprise, and between artistic exploration and promotional exploitation. This phenomenon is particularly devastating to Asian artists who emulate the West without understanding its underlying forces — cultural, social and commercial.

This combination of phenomena has, figuratively speaking, placed Western artists in a culturally weightless state. Hopefully, there exists somewhere a spacecraft of cultural context or an umbilical cord of artistic heritage that may have been programmed to land these free-floating artists on some solid ground in the future. But, alas, the same is not to be for Asian artists who blindly emulate their Western colleagues, having lost their own heritage and thrown away their own legacies. Are they not programmed to self-destruct? Contrary to the easy acceptance of the argument that roots are no more necessary in the modern world comes the rude revelation that the so-called "modern world" is in fact the fruit of creativity in Western culture — albeit with periodic ingestion of creativity from other cultures.

Sharing of modern civilization requires honest and genuine contribution, which can only come from roots that have been nurtured by cultural evolution and creative input over the centuries. As for the revitalization of one's own culture, the beautiful flowers plucked from a neighbour's garden will never set roots for future blossoms. The hypothetical "global culture" as many envision cannot offer a vista larger than the view through the window of whichever society claiming it. At this time, "globalization" simply means "Americanization," and "commercialization" — a reality Europeans have understood better than Asians.

So, then, what is culture? And what does creativity mean? In the West, culture is generally understood as a society's heritage in the way of life. In Asia it may have a more specific meaning. In China, the earliest reference to culture is probably the term *ren wen* 人文 found in the *Yi Jing* 《易經》, which means approximately the "arts of humanity." It is one of the three dimensions of the Chinese universe: heaven, earth and humanity. It supposedly embodies all that is of the highest value to the society, and interacts with the other two: the spiritual and philosophical (*tian wen* 天文) and the environmental and the ecological (*di wen* 地文). Creativity is the source of this mobility. And, this mobility is perhaps very close to the meaning of *dao* 道 in Chinese philosophy, as Zhuangzi stated "that which moves among things is *dao* 行於萬物者道也." And Confucius was quoted in *Lun Yu* 《論語》 (*The Analects of Confucius*) as saying "aiming at *dao*, moving among the arts 志於道，游於藝." Thus, in creativity, as in learning, one must achieve *dao*, the ultimate truth or the supreme understanding. The path to truth is always difficult. But, in the ancient Chinese concept, only truth can give birth to creativity, as Liu Zongyuan 柳宗元 wrote, "arts are to illuminate *dao* 文者以明道義." Deprived of creativity, all cultures decline and become inert, and ultimately fossilized.

The meaning of creativity is, however, illusive. Also, it is not universal. In the modern West, it suggests innovation, invention or even novelty. An artist is often called a "creator" — a lofty title — but is not expected to shoulder specific responsibilities. In traditional Asia, it is hard to find a term equivalent to the modern Western sense of "creativity." Among Chinese classic texts, the closest equivalent is the reference to "a person with true knowledge initiates things 知者創物," in the classic on "crafts," *Kao Gong Ji* 《考工記》. But the real meaning of creativity may well be in the meaning of *dao*, as cited earlier. And the *Dao De Jing* 《道德經》 defines *dao* as "that which gives birth to things 道生之."

Artists and scholars in the East were generally regarded as the conscience of society, and conveyor of its legacy. In ancient China the artist — *wen ren* 文人 or "the person with the ultimate knowledge of the arts 有文德之人." — was simultaneously a scholar or scientist, a statesman, as well as an artist accomplished in a variety of artistic media. As the qualifications for *wen ren* actually approximate that for *sheng ren* 聖人, or the sage, we might assume what is expected of the latter may also apply to the former, the Chinese artist. The *Lushi Chunqiu* 《呂氏春秋》 states that "the sage is deeply concerned about society 聖人深慮人效," while the *Yi Jing* quotes from Confucius that, "the sage learns from the processes of transformation in nature 天地變化聖人效之." Creativity was therefore a matter of necessity, and meant merely to be a point in the continuum of the cultural evolution. Creativity however was only one of the responsibilities of *wen ren*, the most significant of which was continuing the heritage. However, as it is said in the *Yi Jing*, " when the *dao* reaches the end, it transcends and persists 易窮則變，變則通，通則之." The continuation of heritage is therefore the process of transformation as well as evolution. Or, as Han Yu put it "the process of learning from ancient masters is to study the meaning, not the rhetoric 師其意而不師其辭."

While heritage is the root of creativity, to revitalize the legacy calls for responding to stimuli from beyond as well as within the heritage. One example is the absorption of ideas from Central and South Asia in the period leading to the early Tang dynasty. The other is the cultivation of a painting style founded on the abstract expression of calligraphy during the Song dynasty. For example, the study of *su yue* 俗樂 (popular music) of the Tang dynasty must begin with the interaction between *hu yue* 胡樂 and *qing yue* 清樂 that is between the music of Central Asian origin and the traditional music of the Han dynasty then still preserved in the south. A study of Buddhist stone figures will reveal the slow process of stylistically moving away from Central and South Asian influences, beginning with the Northern Wei dynasty, in the fourth century through the Tang dynasty, until the end of the ninth century. On the other hand, the gradual emergence of the *wen ren* painting style from the Song through Yuan dynasties, and its continuation through the early Qing dynasty, literally till only today, represents another long process of evolution. This time, however, the origin was in the rediscovery of profound artistic resources inherent in the purely Chinese medium of brushwork. Another example would be the

prodigious revival in the early Ming Dynasty, of the tradition of *qin* 琴
(zither) music as practised in the Song. This movement took place in the
early fifteenth century after China was occupied almost a hundred years by
the Mongols. Within decades, this remarkable body of music was established as the most significant and aesthetically most characteristic music of
China.

This process of revitalization by assimilation and introspection is
deeply rooted in the legacy and its slow evolution. If and when the legacy
itself becomes trivialized or forsaken, as is today, this process becomes a
rootless emulation of other cultures. True, Chinese culture, as cultures
elsewhere, has experienced periodic declines. It is important to note,
however, that Chinese heritage did not disintegrate between the Han
and Tang dynasties, Tang and Song, or Song and Ming. On the contrary,
Chinese arts flourished in the south throughout the period of the Southern
and Northern Dynasties. Similarly, during the very short Five Dynasties
period, Chinese culture was again well sheltered in the south. The two
Tatar dynasties, the Liao and Jin, which existed concurrently with the
Song, are of major proportions in Chinese history. The Mongol dynasty,
the Yuan, lasting less than a century, allowed the Song heritage to continue
in the late fourteenth century to that of the Ming dynasty, which as in the
case of the Song, was another renewal of Han culture.

It was in the late Ming, at the beginning of the seventeenth century that
Chinese culture began its downward spiral until today, meaning Chinese
culture has been on the decline for a third of the past millennium. True, at
the inception of the Qing dynasty, notable artistic activity did take place,
thanks to the patronage of early Qing rulers. But, fundamentally the arts of
Qing never ventured beyond the tradition of Ming. The Man 滿 rulers came
from a culture that had already been much sinocized and therefore were
without cultural resources of their own to ignite once again a cultural
interaction that could have led to a period of revitalization.

This period of stagnation and disintegration coincided with the rise of
European powers in Asia and colonialism. Western culture came to China
following political and economic gains by European powers. Thus, what
could have been a period of provocation between the cultures of China and
Europe, became instead a one-sided incursion, with Chinese culture too
enfeebled to respond. Long before the Opium War, ethnic and social
injustice, political incapacity, corruption and a deteriorating society had
joined to devastate the empire of the Man rulers. Subsequent invasions,
rebellions, revolutions, civil wars, and political struggles, in addition to

waves of powerful cultural influence from abroad, left the millennia-old Chinese culture in a void. I still remember in the mid-1930s, after a classroom discussion of the text of Liang Qichao's *The History of the Past Hundred Years of China* 《中國近百年史》 the whole class broke down in tears. Today, few would understand why we wept. Even fewer, I imagine, would care about where Chinese cultural heritage has gone. We have lost the memory of our culture.

In all of Asia, heritage has drastically declined since the onset of colonialism. Creativity in the East is now equated with imitation of the West. Worse, commercialized entertainment from the West is mistaken for creative expression in the East, compounding the effect of loss of cultural memory. This is especially unfortunate at a time when cultural diversity is the only means to counteract the sweepingly homogenizing effect of economic globalization.

Asia needs to emphasize continuation as well as development in culture. Without a resurrected heritage, the current surge of creativity in Asia is a drain on its talent and false manifestation of its cultural capacity. When legacies are vibrant again, imitation will give way to assimilation, and creativity will once again be the source of renewal. Only then, the richness of these revivified cultures will interact with Western cultures, leading to a genuinely global new era.

As mentioned earlier, in the past ten years, the Center for United States-China Arts Exchange had been working in Yunnan on its minority cultures. The survival of indigenous and regional cultures today must be recognized in the same way we perceive the survival of "endangered species" in nature. On a global basis, with the successive advent of "Westernization," "industrialization," "modernization," and now "globalization," all indigenous, regional, and even major non-Western cultures are likely doomed as "endangered cultures," unless successful "survival" plans are put in place. But no survival is possible if the formula for salvation is static. Conceptually, the terms of "preservation" and "conservation" are not viable when applied to culture. This is why we have adopted the expression, "continue and develop," a literal translation of the Chinese term *ji cheng fa zhan* 繼承發展, the only viable concept, in our view, to secure survivability for "endangered cultures." Namely, such cultures can flourish only if their "continuation" and "development" take place in tandem.

Among our projects in Yunnan is a new arts department for the teaching of indigenous music, dance, visual arts and crafts. This department recruits masters from the villages to engage in short-term teaching at the department, while the department's students, as well as the faculty travel to the villages periodically to study with local masters in situ and conduct research with the village cultural conveyors. This results in a multi-layered system of mentorship and apprenticeship, and benefits not only the students and faculty, but also the masters and their communities.

Another project, for example, is a group for fieldwork and research to be conducted in village communities in collaboration with revered informants, who are in fact indigenous scholars and cultural leaders. The group further interacts with village communities to promote community-based mentorship and cultural studies. An essential collateral benefit of these projects, as intended in our design, is that the voice of advocating local heritage as a force in community development is now beginning to resonate through every village in Yunnan. Jointly these projects have begun to effectively bring our message to every corner of Yunnan.

The success of our projects in Yunnan has depended on the dedication and knowledge of the participants: scholars, faculty, master artists, or cultural conveyors of one kind or another. These are the people who will revitalize and develop the indigenous cultures of Yunnan. They are potentially the *wen ren* of today, true leaders of their society. China, and all Asia, needs *wen ren* like them.

The term *wen hua* 文化, which is commonly used in modern times for culture, originally meant "education through the arts." Indeed, education in Chinese history has always been at the core of resurrection of legacy or dissemination of initiative. The Chinese classical education system was unique in history. At its best, this system aims at inspiring the students to become *wen ren*, so as to serve society. According to Zhou Dunyi, "sincerity is the essence of a sage 誠者聖人之本." And Li Ao added, " the sage is the first to become aware of what must be accomplished 聖人者人之先覺者也." Since the late nineteenth century, with the disintegration of traditional society in China, there have been repeated reforms in education in Chinese-speaking societies. Heavily influenced by the West, Japan and Soviet Russia, these reforms have consistently reduced the learning of Chinese culture in the curriculum. How can we expect creativity when Chinese arts, literature, philosophy and even history are forsaken at university and pre-college levels.

Without a fundamental curricular restructure, creativity will remain a borrowed procedure, in which aspiration, inspiration and realization are all either Western or Westernized. How can cultures spurred by such creativity be modern Asian or a synthesis of the East and West? Educational overhaul is not only needed for the arts. It is needed across the board. Our work in Yunnan highlights the role of education and research as the first step to cultural revitalization and development. We urgently need courses and research in Asian humanities by Asian educators in Asian societies for their own students.

Let me tell you a story that took place ten years ago. Despite heavy responsibilities in different disciplines at Columbia University, I was pressured by a group of humanities professors to design a "humanities" course on Asian music, complementing an established course on Western music. After its successful installation in the University's course offering for college undergraduates, I was publicly denounced by some senior faculty members of my own department, as a "traitor" — a traitor to Western humanities, of course. I was proud to have set up such a course, probably for the first time in the United States or in the West, and disregarded the shocking slur. But I was more confounded that at that time, because to my knowledge, such a course did not exist in any of the Chinese-speaking societies.

I have already referred to the significance of research in working on Yunnan cultures. I might add another personal experience in that I would not have composed anything personally satisfying without the research that I have done. There is so little living Han legacies known or available to artists of Han heritage. The Song philosopher Chen Yichuan wrote, "If one's knowledge is deep, one will arrive at one's goals 知之深者則行之必至," and "suddenly there appears the opening that leads one through 脫然自有貫通處." Such instant enlightenment comes only through knowledge. This is not uniquely Chinese. Take my profession. Among the twentieth century giants in music, there is hardly one who is not deeply rooted in his own heritage. Varèse, the most radical of them all, was phenomenal in his knowledge of and love for the great music of the past. Bartok was not only a noted pianist of West European music but also the first research scholar of East European musical cultures. And Debussy late in life called himself a "French musician," wishing to redefine what French music meant in his time through his later compositions. All of them exhibited the *wen ren* spirit and would have been accepted by early Chinese sages as one of their own. As for Asian creative artists of the twentieth century, I noted that there are a few exceptions, who can match the above, at least in principle. Jose Maceda of the Philippines is an ethnomusicologist who has always been conducting fieldwork and research in addition to composing. His spirit has deeply influenced the younger generation in his country.

The *wen ren* spirit is at once Chinese and universal — Chinese in that it was a unique situation responsible for more than two millennia of China's cultural and social life; universal in that it stands for commitment to true quality and deep sincerity, to independence, honesty and courage. But, as in the case of any culture or society, *wen ren* spirit also had its ups and downs through the centuries. Faring badly during the Qing Dynasty, its spirit collapsed along with society under the Man rulers. Totally discredited by the early twentieth century, it took much of the blame for the failure of the Qing dynasty. With revolutionary zeal, the *wen ren* spirit was lumped together with everything else labelled superstitious and corrupt, including not only religious beliefs but also Confucius, the *yin-yang* philosophy, and all else that sustained thousands of years of Chinese civilization. They were discarded to free the Chinese people from their shackles in order to embrace the "scientific outlook" of the modern West and to pursue "Westernization." The *wen ren* spirit vanished.

To discuss the psychology of Chinese intellectuals in the 1920s and why this venerable cultural institution could have plunged into oblivion during the Qing would vastly exceed the scope of this speech and my professional competence. I have already ventured beyond the boundaries of my discipline, attempting only to provide an appropriate backdrop for discussion on the nature of the Chinese concept of *wen ren*, and the historic role of *wen ren* in the service of culture.

I would like to note here that the beginning of stagnation of *wen ren* spirit in late Ming coincided with the emergence of modern Europe out of the Renaissance. Similarly, the collapse of the *wen ren* spirit during Qing paralleled the industrialization and expansion of colonial power. There appears to be a causal relationship between *wen ren* and the society at large. That the Mongols failed to bring new artistic stimuli needed for cultural interaction with the Han people they conquered caused China to miss an opportunity for cultural renewal. The brief Mongol rule over China might also have caused the *wen ren* to be preoccupied with returning to the tradition of the Song and earlier periods rather than working towards aesthetic assimilation of other cultures. This period of introspection followed a similar period, the Southern Song, by less than a century. Perhaps such successive, lengthy periods of restoring the past doomed the *wen ren* and thereby the culture of China.

There was little innovation of significance even at the height of the

Ming. and even less in the Qing. Today, the picture turns out to be just the opposite. The influx from abroad is overwhelming. On the other hand, very little of living Chinese culture exists to interact with the flood of creative ideas from abroad, resulting in paradoxically the same thing — no innovation, only imitation.

We noted that the arts in the West currently appear in a weightless state. While the present condition seems to be the trend of the times, we know in the United States, at least, such trends do not last long before they are replaced. On the other hand, the circumstances for this condition, as noted before, are similar to those of earlier periods of cultural change in the West, such as the Renaissance. Recognizing that the Renaissance was contemporaneous to the Ming Dynasty, we should be aware of the fact that the beginning of the decline of Chinese civilization coincided with the inception of ascendancy in Europe. By the time the Byzantine Empire had collapsed, European culture was mature enough to benefit from ideas and events emanating from beyond its boundaries. The rest of the world was unaware of the historic cultural change and incapable of proactive participation, and consequently suffered the predictable fate of not being able to influence the outcome of cultural change or to escape from being a hapless victim.

If change comes, and it may well have already begun, what is the future for Asia? Are the societies of Asia prepared to participate in the change, to interact with the West on the future of such change? Asians do have a choice. They can join the globalization process and become assimilated. Or, they may become partners who have a cultural capital of their own to contribute, so that they do not lose their own identity and will be able to influence the outcome of the change. To achieve that status requires revitalizing the heritage that is so different from that of the West. To breathe new life into the abandoned heritage, commitment of the whole society is necessary. In the East, at least in Chinese-speaking societies, it is time to revive a modern version of the *wen ren* spirit. Once that spirit permeates the arts, research, education, and society — perhaps even commerce and politics, legacies will spring back to life interacting with modern Western heritage, much as yin and yang mingle and beget the future. My own conviction and my experience in Yunnan tells me the future is in a modern *wen ren* spirit, not only for Han Chinese, but for all Asians.

Then and only then, will a new era arrive in Asia, as well as, in the West. A new era, not of globalization, but of global partnership founded on global interaction in culture.

Quantum Listening: From Practice to Theory (To Practise Practice)

Pauline Oliveros

Through the practice of meditation we can explore the depth of insight through the wisdom of listening and hearing. Sogyal Rinpoche[1]

From childhood I have practised listening.

As a musician, I am interested in the sensual nature of sound, its power of synchronization, coordination, release and change. Hearing represents the primary sense organ — hearing happens involuntarily. Listening is a voluntary process that through training and experience produces culture.

All cultures develop through ways of listening.

"Deep Listening" is listening in every possible way to everything possible to hear no matter what you are doing. Such intense listening includes the sounds of daily life, of nature, or one's own thoughts as well as musical sounds.

Deep Listening represents a heightened state of awareness and connects to all that there is. As a composer I make my music through Deep Listening.

Deep Listening is active.

What is heard is changed by listening and changes the listener and I call this the "listening effect" or how we process what we hear. Two modes of listening are available — focal and global. When both modes are utilized and balanced there is connection with all that there is. Focal listening garners detail from any sound and global listening brings expansion through the whole field of sound.

Listening shapes culture locally and universally.

Listening is directing attention to what is heard, gathering meaning, interpreting and deciding on action.

"Quantum listening" is listening to more than one reality simultaneously.

Listening for the least differences possible to perceive perception at the edge of the new. Jumping like an atom out of orbit to a new orbit —

creating a new orbit — as an atom occupies both spaces at once one listens in both places at once. Mothers do this. One focuses to a point and changes that point by listening.

Quantum Listening is listening in as many ways as possible simultaneously — changing and being changed by the listening.

I see and hear life as a grand improvisation: I stay open to the world of possibilities for interplay in the quantum field with self and others, community, society, the world, the universe, and beyond.

Our improvisations will soon include accelerated artificial evolution — hybrid humans (new beings born of technology), new challenges, consequences, dangers, freedoms and responsibilities — all of this in addition to the life we lead through the habits of our own traditions.

How will we meet the genius of more rapidly evolving interactive cultures, a genius of culture that could give us freedom of perception, freedom from physical and mental limitations?

Will we stop the evolution with destruction and annihilation or embrace it courageously to go forward into the new world we are creating with all its edges?

Here follows a brief history and description of my practice called Deep Listening. I also describe Quantum Listening, a theory derived from the practice of Deep Listening. My composing, performing and educating is rooted in my practice and theory.

My theory of Quantum Listening leads back to practise practice!

As a composer and performer I have experienced a relationship with music technology that spans more than half the century. Technology is changing and changing cultures more rapidly now than ever before. What used to take three hundred years now happens in twenty minutes.

The time span of my teaching stretches fifty years from the first lessons I taught to my accordion students at age fifteen to the more recent graduate composition seminars that I have given at Mills College as Darius Milhaud Professor, at Oberlin Conservatory as professor of composition, and in other institutions.

Teaching has always engaged me, given back to me generously, and nourished my career as a composer/performer.

When I taught The Nature of Music to large classes of non-music majors at the University of California at San Diego I wanted to engage the students in creative sound experiences. I began to compose pieces that would allow anyone to participate whether they could read music or not. By 1970 I had begun to compose *Sonic Meditations*,[2] pieces based on the structure of human attention. *Sonic Meditations* gave my work a whole new direction. I began to understand just how important listening is to creative music making. Compared to reading and writing relatively little attention is given to developing listening skills or even to considering the nature of listening.

I have been training myself to listen with a very simple meditation since 1953 when my mother gave me a tape recorder for my twenty-first birthday. The tape recorder had just become available on the home market and was not ubiquitous as it is today. I immediately began to record from my apartment window whatever was happening. I noticed that the microphone was picking up sounds that I had not heard while the recording was in progress. I said to myself then and there:

"Listen to everything all the time and remind yourself when you are not listening."

I have been practising this meditation ever since with more or less success. I still get the reminders after forty-six years. My listening continues to evolve as a lifelong practice.

How we listen creates our life. Listening is the basis of all culture.

The quality and flexibility of listening skills is the foundation of musicianship. The essence of musicianship is the ability to discern the least change in pitch or tempo and relate that discernment to a field of ongoing sound or musical relationships.

For audiences the greatest gift is rapt attention.

Composing *Sonic Meditations* led me deeper into my listening practice and to the notion that there were other important ways to relate to teaching that were different from the presentation to students of prescribed and measurable content. *Sonic Meditations* helped me devise ways to engage students in creative sound making. Processing the results with discussion led to content that came from the inside out (student to professor) rather than exclusively from the outside in (professor to student).

As my work progressed in composition and performance I came to the notion of Deep Listening. In 1988, together with Stuart Dempster and Panaiotis, we made a recording in an underground cistern in Washington State. The recording was released in 1989 by New Albion (NA 022 CD) under the title *Deep Listening*.[3] Quoting from my CD liner notes:

> Each composer represented in Deep Listening has a very individual style of composition. As we improvise together, and listen intensely to one another, our styles encounter in the moment, and intermingle to make a collective music. I call the result *deep listening.*

After I had written these words, many activities began to unfold as *deep listening.*

In 1990 I published *Deep Listening Pieces,*[4] which contains a brief explanation of my listening theory. It involves two attention processes — focal and global listening, and the interdependence of the two modes.

In 1991 together with Heloise Gold, *Tai Ji* master and choreographer, I created and led the first Deep Listening Retreat at Rose Mountain Retreat Center.[5] I had already done research at the Center for Music Experiment at the University of California San Diego in 1973 and given numerous workshops based on my *Sonic Meditations.* This research is detailed in several articles in my book *Software for People.*[6]

The retreat form I devised gave me a wonderful opportunity to focus the material and to work more intensively with people. After five years it was clear that advanced work was needed for those returning each year.

Poet and psychotherapist Ione joined Deep Listening as an instructor to offer Listening Through Dreaming[7] giving the participants the opportunity to practise listening in the retreat twenty-four hours a day.

Based on a request from one of the participants, I decided to offer an advanced retreat and a Three Year Certificate[8] programme for those who would like to teach Deep Listening and use it as a guide for their own creative development.

As a team, Ione, Heloise Gold and I unify our teaching with listening.

Consilient common ground creates a whole learning situation. The retreat is always held in a beautiful natural mountain environment. *Tai Ji* and *Qi Gong* inform and ground the body in the ancient way of the *dao.* Dream incubation and processing bring the aura of dreams into interplay with waking consciousness; sounding and responding through deep listening provide new portals to creativity, unity with self and others.

What is Deep Listening?

For me, Deep Listening is a lifelong practice. The more I listen the more I learn to listen. Deep Listening involves going below the surface of what is heard, expanding to the whole field of sound while finding focus. This is the way to connect with the acoustic environment, all that inhabits it, and all that there is.

For others, Deep Listening is a practice consisting of listening and sounding exercises and pieces I and others have composed since 1970. The results are processed by group discussions in workshops and retreats.

Deep Listening is for musicians as well as participants from other disciplines and interests. Previous musical training is not required.

The key to multilevel existence is Deep Listening — listening in as many ways as possible to everything that can possibly be heard all of the time. Deep Listening is exploring the relationships among any and all sounds whether natural or technological, intended or unintended, real, remembered or imaginary. Thought is included.

Deep Listening includes all sounds expanding the boundaries of perception. This concept includes language and the nature of its sound as well as natural sound and technological sound. In addition, Deep Listening includes the environmental and atmospheric context of sound.

Listening is the key to performance.

Whatever the discipline, responses that originate from Deep Listening resonate with *being*— inform the artist and audience and make art an effortless harmony. Inclusiveness is essential to the process of unlocking layer after layer of imagination, meaning and memory down to the cellular level of human experience.

Hearing is the passive basis of listening.

Hearing is involuntary. Hearing protects us from unseen dangers. We can hear without listening (Unconsciousness). We choose to listen inwardly or outwardly to the past, present or future (Consciousness). Listening actively directs one's attention to what is heard, to the interaction of the relationships of sounds and modes of attention.

We hear in order to listen.

We listen in order to interpret our world and experience meaning. Our world is a complex matrix of vibrating energy, matter and air just as we are made of vibrations. Vibration connects us with all beings and connects us to all things interdependently.

We open in order to listen to the world as a field of possibilities and we listen with narrowed attention for specific things of vital interest to us in the world.

We interpret what we hear according to the way we listen.

Through accessing many forms of listening we grow and change whether we listen to the sounds of our daily lives, the environment or music.

Deep Listening takes us below the surface of our consciousness and helps to change or dissolve limiting boundaries.

Babies are the best Deep Listeners.

Think of the tremendous acts of attention and concentration that babies make to explore sounds and speak their first words, to learn language and communicate through listening.

Deep Listening is a birth right for all healthy humans.

As a blind person the musician Stevie Wonder has listening abilities that persons with normal sight don't ordinarily develop.

Stevie Wonder is a Deep Listener as many blind people are.

With heightened listening ability one can detect the slightest differences in sounds. This enables acute voice recognition, echo detection, spatial location, etc. Such heightened listening substitutes auralization for visualization (or seeing) by creating sonic pictures, etc.

If you are a blind person, hearing is your means of sight, but such acute listening ability also could be cultivated among people with normal sight.

If you were a deaf person hearing for the first time with a newly implanted bionic ear, how would you know what you were hearing? You would have to learn to interpret the sounds.

What if you could hear like a bat zipping and swooping around the night sky, or a whale sounding the depths of the oceans, or elephants sounding the earth?

What would it be like to attend a live concert with the ability to hear it anyway that you like?

What if you as a sophisticated listener could individually adjust and optimize the room acoustics for the music to your own taste?

What if you could equalize and mix an orchestra the way you want to hear it — while other listeners are hearing their own versions of the same concert?

What if you could cancel out any interference automatically so that only the music is purely audible?

What if such feats are possible as an internal and private experience? How could your experience be valued in relation to a community of interest?

What if your experience could be shared instantly in the present moment or later?

Audio engineers already do this; they have developed the art of recording concerts and usually have the best seat in the house for sound which they hear through head phones or near field speakers. The results of their listening can be shared through recordings.

All the technology for controlling the sound of concert acoustics exists already.

What if you could hear the frequency of colours?

Research on visual simulations and robotic sight has far outpaced research on hearing. Hearing has not seemed as important to scientists and technologists as seeing. One hears repeatedly that we live in a "visually oriented society" even though the ear tells the eye where to look.

Those of us who are aurally-oriented are marginalized.

For example: The recent 165 million dollar Mars probe launched by NASA had a 15 dollar microphone from a hearing aid module along as a hitchhiker. This was an afterthought although listening for the sounds of other worlds could yield data that might not come from cameras. We take cameras to the zoo, not tape recorders. And zoos are generally not open during prime sound time in the early morning or evening.

We need to be listening in all possible modes to meet the challenges of the unknown — the unexpected.

An unconscious negative attitude that makes hearing less important than sight developed in parallel with industrial age technology. Pre-industrial cultures depended on hearing for survival needs. Now unnecessarily loud motor sounds serve to let the operator know that a machine is working. Silent machines are possible but people seem to need the aural feedback even though it may contribute to the destruction of their hearing.

Why is industrial sound so often excessive?

Sound conveys a sense of power and connection to the machine operator. Sound is the mythos and symbolic representation of the need to accumulate power. It is unconscious "participation mystique." The sounds of machines dominate and are a constant ubiquitous presence.

There is no courting of silence.

Urban sound levels continue to rise in a great cacophonic puzzle.

Those who operate machines can feel powerful — in control.

No part of the planet is untouched by machine sound. No wonder that Youth Culture has embraced loud amplified music. How else could they feel heard, extending their work to audiences as a powerful presence?

Technology has deeply altered the quality of life, both positively and negatively.

The devaluation of hearing through unconsciousness and ignorance has caused a serious imbalance in the quality of life. Suppression of listening is a consequence of this imbalance. Separation and alienation results. How we attend to this imbalance will have a profound influence on the future of human values. How we use the power of sound and music affects our values.

We need sound designers and composers as consultants to city planning and noise abatement regulation.

Machines such as cranes, earth movers, pile drivers, etc. have amplified human muscle power enormously in the Industrial Age and enabled the large building accomplishments in the development of cities. We have machines that multiply and leverage our senses and our mental capabilities. In the twenty-first century we will be grappling with who we are as extended humans — hybrid computer/humans and computer beings.

We already see and hear far into outer space and into micro space.

With the Hubble telescope we are able to see into galaxies from the edge of the universe. How thrilling it would be if we could also hear this too. How about launching a parabolic microphone on the next satellite to listen for the music of the spheres? With the electron microscope we can see atomic structures, but we could also listen to the micro-world, hearing a strange universe unfolded by quantum mechanics.

Research on hearing and repairing damaged ears increased after World War II, whereas the need for ear protection in the work place had not been recognized earlier. Hearing loss is usually a slow painless process occurring over many years and not necessarily detected until late in its progression. When veterans returned from battle with acoustic trauma, the more instant damage from the loud explosions of war motivated the Army to do new research on protecting and repairing ears.

In 1978 the first person was implanted with a bionic ear. Rod Saunders went profoundly deaf because of head injury, and received a bionic ear when he was 48 years old. The prototype bionic ear (a cochlear transplant) proved to be a success and was commercialized in 1982. A range of improvements over the years as a result of the continuing research has led to additional benefits for people like Rod. Now over 20,000 people throughout the world can hear because of the bionic ear, including over 10,000 children.[9]

At least 28 million people in the United States suffer hearing loss. 60 percent have genetic hearing loss and the rest have damaged ears from industrial noise and loud music. At least 16 million are under thirty years old.[10]

Ignorance (more than accidents) causes ear damage which is currently irreversible. All the devices that are supposed to contribute positively to the quality of life are dangerous if they also produce sound levels at and above 85db and people have more or less continuous exposure to those levels.

Many people especially young people have not a clue as to the danger of loud music through head phones, or at a disco, or concert.

People are not necessarily aware of the occupational hazards of loud motors although some progress has been made. Workplace ethics should hold employers accountable for such hazardous sound. Manufacturers should be accountable too.

Musicians need education about the dangers of their profession.

Audiologists should be consulted routinely and should hold positions as health inspectors. Just as restaurants must maintain cleanliness against infectious microbes, industrial workplaces should be free of continuous sound above 85db. Ear protection should be provided for employees.

Interpretation of our sense information (listening) and the sharing of this experience with each other is the basis of culture and our values.

For example, the members of traditional musical ensembles share knowledge through the experience of performing together, interpreting and creating repertoire and sharing it with audiences. Audiences participate by responding to the music. We rejoice in the pleasure of music that we know and love. Community develops around music. Critical response, discernment and education help to shape and conserve musical values.

Unfamiliar contemporary music tests values, challenges habits, helps to create new thought patterns and expanded awareness. We need an improvatory of music[11] to balance the conservatory and promote the creation of music.

The Youth Culture "Generation" is transforming music and creating new values across cultural divides. DJs are remixing the artifacts of recorded music cultures as performances. They are listening differently. They are deconstructing recorded music and turning recorded sound into live performance. The movement is powerful and reaches others instantly through the Internet as well as other media venues. Their listening and cultural flexibility is the future of music.

My own work is now presented live on the Internet. Fifty years ago I performed for the first time on another new media venue — television. Now in the twenty-first century the Youth Culture will navigate this new Internet venue.

We have arrived at the threshold of the twenty first century with sense organs developed gradually by natural selection through the slow millennial process of evolution. We assume that as humans we hear in the same manner although not all ears have the same acuity. And, because we do not all share the same culture, we definitely are not all listening in the same way with the same attention.

Soon we will be faced with an unprecedented exponential acceleration in technology.

How do we understand normal hearing? What are we listening for?

Restoration of damaged sense organs and nerves will be possible. Regeneration of nerves may be possible also. For the first time there also may be a choice for enhancement of sense organs and for new perceptual abilities if our brains can handle the processing involved with the unfamiliar. When we cannot process complex information we tend to shut down our senses and retreat.

What if such retreat were impossible?

What if we could share our thoughts instantly over a network as computers now do? Such possibilities and amplified intelligence will present new challenges to our ethics and future human values.

What would you want to hear if you had a Bionic Ear that could let you listen to anything, anywhere any time?

As a musician would you like to focus on a particular instrument in an orchestra that seems inaudible? Or listen globally with the ability to equalize and optimize the sound of the whole ensemble canceling out any distracting interferences?

What does a bat hear as it swoops and dives through the air sounding its prey to locate it?

Would you like to zoom into a waterfall to hear individual sounds of the falling drops? Would you like to hear the sound of a cell dividing in your own body? The sound of blood coursing through your veins as you monitor your own health?

How about discerning the exact distance of sounds with an internal molecular computer?

What are the sounds of the gases in deep space?

All of this enhancement to hearing is already available with outboard equipment — microphones, amplifiers, speakers.

Surveillance by spies is quite sophisticated.

What if such equipment were available as on board internal equipment through microscopic ingested technology? (Never mind implants — they will be outdated.) How would you want to use your newly-enhanced ear power? How could humanity handle such power?

What is microscopic ingested technology?

According to Raymond Kurzweil "Nanobots are microscopic sized robots which will exist by 2030."[12] Entering the blood stream nanobots could scan your brain from the inside. Nanobots could swim through every capillary of your brain and take a high-resolution picture from inside.

Note that Kurzweil doesn't posit nanobots that listen.

Nanotechnology is underway. The result could mean that new neural networks could be created and controlled within the brain. Nerves could be repaired. Brain extenders could extend your pattern recognition and memory. You would have the processing power of powerful computers or return to normal carbon based being.

Kurzweil predicts that

> In a hundred years there may be no clear distinction between humans and computers. There will be enormous augmentation of human perceptual and cognitive abilities through neural implant technology. Humans who do not use such implants (or nanobots) are unable to participate in meaningful dialogue with those who do — knowledge is understood instantaneously through assimilated knowledge protocols. The goal of education and intelligent beings is discovering new knowledge to learn.[13]

What about spirituality?

To Kurzweil a spiritual experience is "a pattern of information."[14]

For Matthew Fox

> Spirituality by definition means plummeting to the depths, getting down to the realm of experience. Spirituality is about living deeply. It puts experience before everything else. It's about responding with passion, awe, reverence and gratitude to everything in life — including the grief, the pain, the suffering, the injustice. It's about tasting God, not just talking about God.[15]

We will need all the wisdom that we can possibly absorb to deal morally and ethically with the powers inherent in nanotechnology. Our battles with good and evil will jump to a new level.

Enter the Chip Monk![16] Will spirituality evolve on a microchip with the programmed essence of the best of our world religions available to all? Could the Chip Monk be ingested to assist one's inner monk in the practice of deep ecumenism and the distillation of universal truth?

If you are a Buddhist listening leads to the "Buddhaverse;" if you are a Christian listening leads you to the word of God; if you are an artist listening leads you to your material and to shape the material; if you are a scientist listening leads you to theory and experiment.

If you are a spy listening may lead you to prison.

Quantum Listening leads you to notice that you are listening. Quantum Listening leads you to attention to a point — all or nothing focus which changes that point forever.

Quantum Listening leads you to an all-embracing perspective of an ever-expanding field.

We live in these conditions and our listening simultaneously perceives and shapes the moments that we live whether we are Buddhist, Christian, Islamic, Artist, scientist etc. Whoever and whatever we are, religion is a set of rules and regulations for a particular kind of listening. Style in art sets the way of listening.

Quantum Listening is listening to our listening. The field expands to embrace all kinds of listening with openness to all possibilities.

In 1990 the noted ethnomusicologist Ki Mantle Hood proposed the Quantum Theory of Music. When asked for the formula for QTM in 1994 he replied: "At present, our modus operandi is asking questions. We try to identify neglected, overlooked, not-always-obvious phenomena that relate in any way to the perception of music. That order of perception is only possible by participation."[17] Participation means actually experiencing all aspects of music creation and performance.

What is Quantum Listening?

Quantum Listening is listening in all sense modes to or for the least possible differences in any component part of a form or process while perceiving the whole and sensing change.

The Quantum Listener listens to listening.

Quantum Listening simultaneously creates and changes what is perceived. The perceiver and the perceived co-create through the listening effect. All sounds are included in the field. This creates potential, cultivates surprises, opens the imagination, and approaches and even plunges over the edges of perception into the mystery of the universe predicted by Quantum Field Theory.

Quantum Listening is the ability to discern all that there is in a single moment — point in space (a transient) or a quantum.

"In the new physics of Quantum Field Theory, particles — have an 'aura' or a force field. Although it cannot be seen, its presence is felt. It conveys forces from one particle to another as they interact."[18]

Analogously when one is listening to the whole field of sound without focusing on any one sound but expanding to include all sounds that can be heard — sounds seem to become interrelated rather than chaotic or mean-ingless — the field conveys forces (energy) from one sound to another.

The field seems to have a unified logic and form, as if it were a composed piece of music.

"What is a field? A field carries the potential for manifesting a force. Particles of objects inside a field may change or move."[19]

The field of sound can be felt as potential force. There is active participation by the listener and co-creation of this form between the listener and sounds.

The field assumes meaning (potential force) and is transformed by the listener.

The listener is also transformed by the field. If one is not listening in this expanded way then the form disappears into the background of consciousness — the field disappears — is meaningless, attention narrows, the potential lessens. This is analogous to the collapse of the wave function in Quantum Mechanics when a particle is observed and decides to change state.

Within the "Listening Field" sounds which shift and change inside the field are the manifestation of forces which give rise to the perceived form. Listeners will hear the form slightly differently, each from their own angle of observation in the field. Different listeners would have to occupy different locations in the field, thus making their experience of the field different. This is no less true when listening to a piece of music in an audience in a concert hall.

A Quantum Theory of Music[20] as proposed in 1990 by Ki Mantle Hood would have to account for these slight differences in perception, their interaction and effect.

Each listener by the act of "listening" affects the field and thus the form. The form affects the listener in a dance of reflections in the space between.

Listening performers feel the "listening effect" as they are performing for an audience.

This is focal/global listening with the added perspective of a "witness" function.

This is listening to listening — layers of processing in the brain and body.

The skin listens too.

In fact the whole body listens in this heightened state of awareness which can expand continually, unless attention narrows (perhaps to ego concerns) and there is the collapse of the wave function and a change in the field and its potential.

In practising *Qi Gong* I have experienced listening with the palms of my hands to sense these electromagnetic fields. Since these are vibrations I call this sensing listening with the palms of the hands. Simply imagining the sound of humming transfers immediately to the palms of my hands and manifests as healing energy.

There is a deep relationship between *Qi Gong* and Quantum Field Theory.

According to the speculation of physicist E. H. Walker,

> Consciousness may be associated with all quantum mechanical processes — since everything that occurs is ultimately the result of one or more quantum mechanical events, the universe is "inhabited" by an almost unlimited number of rather discrete, conscious — entities that are responsible for the detailed workings of the universe[21]

Can sounds be understood as particles?

"In a fashion analogous to auric fields, particle fields influence certain particles when near them."[22]

Sounds near one another influence each other. Listeners near one another affect or influence one another with active listening.

"Particles have auras. This makes them like everything else in the universe, as the ancient Chinese viewed it." (*ibid*).

"Photons (light particles), do appear to process information and to act accordingly, and therefore, strange as it may sound, they seem to be organic"[23]

Particles behave as if they had consciousness.[24]

"In fact, modern Quantum Field Theory suggests that what we call a particle is an 'energy knot' in the field." Thus particles are a flow creating the illusion of a form, made up of concentrated *Qi*. "*Qi* is similar to a cloud."[25]

> "When the *Chi* (*Qi*) condenses, its visibility (*or audibility*) becomes apparent so that there are then the shapes (of individual things [*or sounds*]). When it disperses its visibility (*or audibility*) *is* no longer apparent and there are no shapes (*or sounds*). At the time of its condensation, can one say otherwise than that this was but temporary? But at the time of its dispersing, can one hastily say that it is then non existent?"[26]

Is sound intelligent? Does sound have consciousness?

Listen to sound disappearing. This meditation that I practise takes one to the border of reality and virtuality. When do you stop hearing the sound? When does memory begin?

What we hear depends on the angle from which our ear receives sound. How we listen depends on our consciousness. Are we creating the sound that we hear by listening or is sound creating our listening? Is it co-creation between consciousnesses? Is the sound disappearing or am I disappearing?

Human values are developed through the experience of listening. With practice humanity could be transformed to a flexible culture of listeners.

> Listening involves a reciprocity of energy flow; exchange of energy; sympathetic vibration: tuning into the web of mutually supportive inter-connected thoughts, feelings, dreams, vital forces comprising our lives; empathy; the basis for compassion and love. Yes, Deep Listening is the foundation for a radically transformed social matrix in which compassion and love are the core motivating principles guiding creative decision making and our actions in the world. Quantum Listening is a "simple" practice, open to all, which has profoundly rich and far-flung implications, for bringing to our world the two conditions the Dalai Lama illuminates in his recent book *Ethics for the New Millennium*:[27] happiness and relief of suffering.[28]

The practice generates theory.

Theory is perceiving structure — analyzing and explaining structure so that testing and experiments (practice) can be done. Theory directs practice and creates culture to practise practice.

Practice is a way of action — a set or sets of ways of doing or respond-ing to gain experience.

Listeners practising cultural flexibility[29] would be aware of the pro-found interdependence of all beings and all things. A new music reflective of a new humanity with a high value on life could arise.

[Special Thanks to all Deep Listeners and to H.E. Tai Situ Rinpoche, Monique Buzzarte, Abbie Conant, Stuart Dempster, Lester Ingber, Ione, Norman Lowrey, William Osborne, Jann Pasler, Alex Potts, Moira Roth, Juliet Shepherd, and Bonnie Wright.]

Notes

1. Sogyal Rinpoche, Interview, http://www.comngrnd.com/rinpoche.html.
2. Oliveros, Pauline. *Sonic Meditations*. Urbana, Ill.: Smith Publications, 1974.
3. Dempster, Oliveros, Panaiotis. *Deep Listening*. New Albion (NA 022 CD).
4. Oliveros, Pauline. *Deep Listening Pieces*. Deep Listening Publications, 1990, http://www.deeplistening.org/dlc.
5. Deep Listening Retreat at Rose Mountain, http://www.deeplistening.org/.
6. Oliveros, Pauline. *Software for People*. Urbana, Ill.: Smith Publications, 1984.
7. Ione. *Is This A Dream?* Workshop Manual, 1997, M.O.M.
8. Three Year Certificate program, http://www.deeplistening.org/.
9. Bionic Ear, http ://www.medoto.unimelb.edu.au/bei/history1.htm.
10. National Institutes of Health Consensus Development Conference on Noise and Hearing Loss.

11. Oliveros, Pauline. *Quantum Improvisation: The Cybernetic Presence.* Improvisation Across Borders Conference, UCSD1999, http ://www.artswire. org/pof/quantum.html.

12. Lee, Virginia. *More Perfect Than Man.* Interview with Ray Kurzweil, http:// www.comngrnd.com/.

13. Kurzweil, Ray. *The Age of Spiritual Machines: When Computers Exceed Human Intelligence.* New York: Viking House, 1999.

14. Lee, Virginia, *ibid.*

15. Lee, Virginia, Interview with Matthew Fox, http://www.comngrnd.com/fox. html.

16. Chip Monk was contributed by Dempster, Stuart<dempster@u.washington. edu>.

17. Hood, Ki Mantle, *Quantum Theory of Music,* The Perfect Beat 1990.

18. Petersen, P. Steven, *The Quantum Tai Chi,* Empyrean Quest Publishers, 1996.

19. *Ibid.*

20. Hood, Ki Mantle, *ibid.*

21. Walker Evan Harris, *The Nature of Consciousness.* Mathematical Biosciences, 7, 1970, pp. 131–78.

22. Petersen, P. Steven, *ibid.*

23. Zukav, Gary, *The Dancing Wu Li Masters.* New York Bantam Books, 1979, pp. 63–64.

24. Petersen, P. Steven, *ibid.*

25. Weyl, H., *Philosophy of Mathematics and Natural Science.* [Princeton NJ.: Princeton University Press, 1949. Revised and augmented]. New York: Atheneum Pubs., 1963, p. 171.

26. Quoted in Fung Yu-lan, *A Short History of Chinese Philosophy.* New York: Free Press; London: Macmillan, c. 1948; New York: Macmillan, 1960 [Ed. Derk Bodde], p. 279.

27. Dalai Lama. *Ethics for the New Millennium.* New York: Riverhead Books, 1999.

28. Written by Norman Lowrey, professor of composition Drew University and Deep Listening Certificate holder.

29. *Cultural flexibility* was contributed by Abbie Conant in a conversation with the author.

References

Print

Kurzweil, Raymond (1999). *The Age of Spiritual Machines: When Computers Exceed Human Intelligence.* New York: Viking Press.

Lipsitz, George (1994). *Dangerous Crossroads: Popular Music, Postmodernism and the Poetics of Space.* London; New York: Verso Press.

Mirande, Alfredo (1997). *Hombres y Machos: Masculinity and Latino Culture.* Boulder, Colorado: Westview Press.

Moravec, Hans (1988). *Mind Children: The Future of Robot and Human Intelligence.* Cambridge, Massachusetts: Harvard University Press.

Morris, Richard (1999). *The Universe, the Eleventh Dimension, and Everything We Know and How We Know It.* New York: Four Walls Eight Windows.

Oliveros, Pauline (1998). *The Roots of the Moment.* New York: Drogue Press.

Picard, Rosalind W. (1997). *Affective Computing.* Cambridge, Massachusetts: MIT Press.

Reading, Massachusetts: Addison-Wesley.

Rheingold, Harold (1991). *Virtual Reality.* New York: Summit Books.

—— (1993). "A Slice of Life in My Virtual Community." Linda M. Harasim, ed., *Global Networks: Computers and International Communication.* Cambridge, Massachusetts: MIT Press.

Sagan, Carl (1997). *The Demon Haunted World: Science as a Candle in the Dark.* London: Headline Book.

Sale, Kirpatrick (1995). *Rebels Against the Future: The Luddites and Their War on the Industrial Revolution.* Reading, Massachusetts: Addison-Wesley.

Shils, Edward (1981). *Tradition.* Chicago: University of Chicago Press.

Stock, Gregory (1993). *Metaman: The Merging of Humans and Machines into a Global Organism.* Toronto: Doubleday Canada.

Turkle, Sherry (1996). *Life on the Screen: Identity in the Age of the Internet.* New York: Simon and Schuster.

Wilson, E. O. (1998). *Consilience: The Unity of Knowledge.* New York: Alfred A. Knopf.

Electronic

http://iias.leidenuniv.nl/oidelon/issues/issue2/articies/hood/frame-o.html.

http ://www.zinezone.com/zones/digital/multimedia/kurzweil/interview6.html.

http ://ajanta.sci.ccny.cuny.edu/~jupiter/pub/com/baeparts/superstring.html.

http://www.angelfire.com/hi2/UFOCHARTS/index.html.

http ://msnbc.com/news/202284.asp?cp1=1.

http ://www.neurosonics.com/bgm-kurzweil.html.

http ://www. comngrnd.com/houston.html.

http://www.comngrnd.com/rinpoche.html.

http://www.militaryaudiology.org/bang/index.html Educating Children about Hearing.

http://www.medoto.unimelb.edu.au/bei/history1.htm.

http://www.militaryaudiology.org/aric/index.htm.

Justifying Critical Differences: Which Concepts of Value Are Sustainable in an Expanded Coordination

Laurent Thévenot

Introduction

It is now widely accepted that the globalization process puts a high strain on the present diversity of values which has been produced by a variety of cultures or civilizations. We have two contrasting types of scenario: one is an eventual reduction of this diversity and unification within one outstanding value frame; the other is a possible composition of a plurality of value frames which would support the kind of enlargement of their scope which a global world requires. If we choose to explore the more attractive second scenario, close attention has to be paid to the two distinct problems of composition and enlargement of value frames.

As a matter of fact, these two problems have long been the core of the political constitution of particular societies, before any global extension was debated. To build a "polity" — if we use this term to designate such a political constitution of societies — one has to solve both of these problems: (a) in order to maintain civil peace, a mode of composition should integrate the plurality of goods which the society members are looking for and prevent a violent confrontation; (b) in order to govern the polity, a reference to the public good must enlarge somehow the particular goods and interests which are at stake. Political philosophers were the designers of such constructions of polities. I am particularly concerned here by the "political and moral grammars" which sustain these constructions, and I want to relate them to the problem of coordination between human agents. In the first section, I will recall some of these grammars which govern the kind of agreements and disagreements considered as most legitimate in a polity. The first focuses on collective entities while the second is based on individual ones. I will compare the way each of them fosters, or blocks, a move towards the globalization of human interactions.

Does globalization concern exclusively the kind of human interactions which political philosophy and social sciences usually deal with? I don't think so, considering that globalization is primarily characterized in terms of new communication and market networks which, only in the second phase, affect politics and morals. It then raises a difficult problem for modern political philosophy which is not well prepared to integrate such technical realities. In so-called traditional societies, cosmologies maintained a civil peace which extended far beyond the human community. They aggregate a whole variety of entities to the congregation of human beings. But modern science has monopolized the investigation into the order of nature, its laws and uncertainties. Political and moral philosophy only rescues the enquiry on human order and its troubles. In the second section, I state that we are in great need, nowadays, of political and moral grammars of a new sort, which would enable us to sustain a realist polity, in the sense of its being abundantly furnished and equipped with things of nature and artifice. My contention is that values and goods help to coordinate not only the relations between human beings but also in their commerce with natural or artificial entities of their environment. I submit the grammars which I previously sketched out to the question of their ability to integrate relations with things.

This leads to the third section which introduces a third type of political and moral grammar which I analyzed with Luc Boltanski (Boltanski and Thévenot, 1991).[1] This grammar offers an integration of relations to things and departs significantly from the two above-mentioned models. Our work originated from the empirical study of disputes involving people and things, when people have recourse to most legitimate forms of evaluation to frame their arguments and put them to a test. What we call "orders of worth." Then, we had a new look on a series of political philosophers whom we selected because they adequately captured the construction of each of these orders of worth. As I argue in the fourth and last section, this grammar of worth is a key construction for our present reflection, because it results in the transformation of a variety of local forms of evaluation in order to make them compatible with a requirement of *common humanity*. In addition, each order of worth places value on a mode of relation with our non-human environment while also governing human relationships. The result of a comparative study of repertoires of evaluation in France and the United States (Lamont and Thévenot, 2000) helps to situate the place of these different grammars in contrasted political and moral contexts.

Political and Moral Grammars Coping with Globalization

Looking at Values as Coordinating Devices

My approach to values is the following. I contend that values and similar normative concepts are devices which human societies have crafted to deal with the problematic coordination of human conduct. They serve to frame disputes (not to prevent them) and to find settlements. This perspective on values in use is not confined to contextual interactions or local negotiation. I am concerned by the ways values, or references to the good, support the generalization of arguments and settlements. It allows me to reverse the initial question on the consequences of globalization on a diversity of values. I would rather explore the following question: How do various conceptualizations of values support the kind of enlargement of the scope in the coordination of actions which is required by contemporary societies?

The conception of "modes of coordination" I defend departs from the usual understanding of coordination in the following way. As I view it, coordination articulates two notions which are frequently opposed: the engagement of some *good* and of some *reality*.

On the one hand, practical coordination demands that the agent uses some *form of evaluation* to screen what is most important for them to take into account for their own action. This form of evaluation implies the delineation of some *good*, which might be more or less extended, from an idea of the common good to a notion of private interest. On the other hand, coordination is a practical issue. The form of evaluation is put to a reality test when action is effectively engaged. Thus, my approach links the orientation towards some kind of good to a characterization of the access to reality which leads to some sort of *realism*.

Depending on the ways the good and the reality are treated, agents coordinate their conducts along a variety of pragmatic "regimes of engaging the world," as I coined the notion (Thévenot, 1990, 2001a and 2001b). Here, I shall focus on public regimes which have been specifically devised for the broad coordination of action at distance, not for engaging in familiarity, for instance.

The Constitution of a "Polity" and Its Political and Moral Grammar

Long before any consideration on globalization was raised, the constitution of *polities* had already coped, on a more limited basis, with the issue of legitimate modes of coordinating actions. Viewed in the perspective of coordination, the political and moral grammars which sustain such polities offer specific answers to the following question:

(1) Which are the coordinated entities? How are the members of the polity characterized?   How do they *qualify for* being represented in the polity?

(2) Which is the relevant *good* which is supposed to orient the agents' conduct and their forms of evaluations?

(3) Which *mode of composition* integrates the various types of goods and contribute to the coordination of conduct?

(4) Which *enlargement* of these goods makes the reference of a *public good* possible?

Let us first consider two contrasted political and moral grammars which are frequently involved in the debate over globalizing values.

A Grammar of Community

A first kind of grammar sustains communitarian polities and might be specified with the following features:

(1) Human agents are treated as members of a particular community and closely linked by this common membership; they are better characterized as a collectivity.

(2) The good is a common good for the community; it might be substantially defined; it is expressed through traditions and rituals.

(3) The coordination succeeds because of the alignment of conducts which are made similar by a strong affinity of shared motives. More or less institutionalized conventions enforce this alignment.

(4) The communitarian good is enlarged at the scale of the whole community, though not at a larger scope.

A Grammar of Liberal Democracy

The political grammar of liberal democracy differs from the previous one on each of its main features:

(1) Human agents are viewed as individuals moved by an autonomous will.

(2) The relevant good has the limited scope of the individual agent. The associated form of evaluation is subjective preference. Even

values and references to "common goods" such as altruism are, in this construction, reduced to individual preferences. This individual good is frequently naturalized in terms of a causal interest. Individual goods or interests might be extended to collective interests. But they still remain of the same kind and do not create membership, or strong ties, among individuals who are oriented towards the same good.

(3) The coordination is achieved through the composition of individual goods expressed by individual opinions, and a negotiation between the different interests, stakeholders or lobbies.

(4) The output of this coordination process is a good which has been made public by the composition of a plurality of independent voices.

Putting the Two Grammars to the Test of Globalization

From the previous sketch of the two types of grammars, what can we say regarding the consequences of globalization on each of them?

The first grammar of the community is clearly not well prepared for extension. Membership involves a double attachment to a particular past and to a particular space which solidifies the boundaries of the community and hardens the distinction between those who are within and those who are outside. It raises obstacles for communication across these boundaries. The territorial anchoring also opposes the kind of nomadic detachment which globalization demands. The alignment of conducts is the source of communitarian coordination, but does not help for action and judgment with strangers. Valorization on the basis of common membership might easily lead to ostracism and violent confrontation.

As a result of these features, this first model is generally disqualified when the issue of globalization is at stake. It serves to promote the advantages of the second model, making it to appear as particularly adjusted to a global extension of market and communication exchanges. A third model might actually appear to be even more adequate for a large extension of exchanges, and to combine the benefits both of liberal democracy and of communitarianism, that is: multiculturalism.

The Multicultural Enlargement of the Liberal Grammar

Although there are many versions of multiculturalism, I shall state that this last grammar is generally akin to the second liberal one, while absorbing the first — communitarian — by means of a drastic reduction of the notion of community. The multiculturalist grammar might allow a plurality of communities to find their place in a globalized extension of the polity, following the way they composed more limited immigrant nations. But the reduction has its cost since it transforms communitarian polities into cultural identities.

Social sciences actively cooperated to this political transformation. Ethnologists contributed to obtain equal recognition for the values of most diverse societies, in a brave defense of a universal human nature. The crafting of the notion of culture served the projection of a variety of exotic polities on the same plane, bringing them into an equivalent form and opposing the hierarchical ordering of folks or races. In contemporary politics, this levelling process does not aim at integrating exotic worlds, but at maintaining some coherence in the interior of the polity. The multicultural reduction treats the diversity of communities as a range of identities within which individuals might do their choice for their own benefit, as they do with any other individual good.

The Questionable Realism of Political and Moral Grammars

The comparison of the previous grammars shows that the second and the third ones are much more armed to cope with globalization. In fact, they have already been tested in the composition of immigrant nations. However, several limitations appear in the implementation of these models of polity. I will point to some of them which are related to the two key issues I chose to focus on, in my approach of modes of coordination: the kind of *realism* which the grammar allows and the kind of *good* which may be discussed within this grammar. The two issues converge in a reflection on the notion of critical pluralism that the model sustains.

The Missing Good and Reality of Multicultural Pluralism

In the enlargement of the liberal grammar to multiculturalism, pluralism is achieved with two types of sacrifice. First, it renounces the prospect of comparison and commensuration between the variety of values which are embedded in different cultures. It hinders the reflection on forms of good and evaluation which might overcome, for certain purposes of large-scale coordination, the boundaries between these cultures. Such a reflection is discredited because of its universalistic pretension which is supposed to hide the dominating project of a particular culture. I take seriously the threat of a dominating value and this was the point of departure of my talk. But this threat should not prevent the debate on the kind of goods and evaluations which might be compatible with the recognition of a common humanity. In fact, a closer examination shows that some critical version of a multicultural polity assumes a kind of common good. We called it *civic* good and it aims at a universal quest of equality and solidarity among human beings. This kind of good is the necessary basis for criticizing the abusive domination of one culture on the other, and claiming solidarity in favour of such and such dominated minority.

Hence, the first sacrifice halts the search for general forms of evaluation, or common goods, which could help coordination between human beings beyond their cultural membership or identity. The second sacrifice prevents the exploration of a second important question for our purpose: How do specifications of the common good contribute to the integration of a material reality within a polity. This exploration is crucial for the issue of globalization since we observe that the development of new technology is playing a central role in the transformation and enlargement of polities. Yet multiculturalism is mainly oriented towards beliefs, or symbolic identities. The limitation of pluralism to a tolerant diversity of beliefs entails a default of realism. If a polity is composed by a juxtaposition of incommensurate beliefs, opinions or values, it does not hold on the reality of nature and artifice which constitutes the "furniture," or the equipment of human societies. We see an unhappy consequence of this limitation in the fact that the political and moral issues raised by globalization are viewed as *debatable* while market or communication networks are considered as *causing* the move and, therefore, out of debate.

In fact, the grammar of multiculturalism has affinity with market realism. In continuity with the liberal grammar, it fits well the kind of reality which privately satisfies the good of individuals and allows negotiation between them. The market formatting of reality which shapes market goods espouse the liberal grammar. Cultural identities are thus marketed as other merchandises. In its less radical forms, the grammar of multiculturalism implicitly includes the common good of market competition and the kind of reality which qualifies for price evaluation. This grammar does not offer a critical interplay between a plurality of common goods, nor the possibility to question the over-whelming extension of market.

The Lack of Material Embedding of Political and Moral Grammars

More generally, political and moral grammars rarely pay close atten-tion to the natural and artificial embedding of human communities. Among few notable exceptions, Marx analyzes, in *Capital*, the role of merchandise, exchange value and use value in political economy (Marx, 1887), and Arendt pays careful attention, in *The Human Condi-tion* (1958), to the role played by the environment of human artifacts in the "housing" of individual lives.[2] The most influential model of politi-cal economy conceives politics and morals of human relations with things in the state of commodities. The specific notion of realism which originates in this relation to market goods deeply influenced theories of justice in their views of distributive justice as an individual allocation of scarce resources. I deplore that such theories usually presuppose only one kind of human relations with their environ-ment, while we should account for the variety of these relations in contemporary societies. A realist approach to the questioning on the good should not confine to the allocation of market goods. Once we admit that the various conceptions of the good contribute to the coordination of human beings with their surroundings, we need a more open view on the variety of ways human beings engage with nature and artifice. Unrealistic political grammars leave to the natural sciences the whole burden of dealing with the material world. Opin-ions and values on such contentious issues as genetically modified organisms, or mad cow disease, appear to be weak on many occasions when confronted with scientific statements which monopolize objectivity.

Which Conception of Realist Polities?

Taking things into account usually occurs at a second step, once the political grammar has been built. Many critiques of techniques thus origi-nate in politics and morals which have been devised to govern purely human communities. In a second step, they ask whether the addition of techniques has been advantageous for human communities. I propose to partly reverse these two steps. I shall first consider, from the very beginning of the political and moral enquiry, that human beings are attached to a material environment. I shall even state that moral considerations are built on these attachments. The thrust of the argument is that attachment to things eventually brings asymmetries among human capacities. The perspective of a common human dignity, which remains a principal moral prerequisite, questions the ground or rationale of these asymmetries. The result is a specification of the good which takes into account a certain relation to things.

Attachment to things enhance the capacities of human beings. However, any involvement of things does not immediately triggers the questioning of the good in terms of common humanity, or injustice. A statement about unequal capacities requires that a certain relation to things must be systematically generalized. This is the case, for example, of a systematic relation to things as market goods, or as technical implements, or as signs which support common visibility, or as informational devices, etc. Once generalized, a certain relation to things makes particular situations comparable. Otherwise, they stay too manifold to be comparable and give rise to a shared concern about asymmetrical capacities. Local situations might cause personal uneasiness but do not ease the expression of general statements about injustice or abuse of power. Power is at stake though it cannot constitute an *a priori* category of analysis: its formulation and questioning vary along with the kind of relation to things which is generalized.

Aggrandizing Reality and Values

Values and Systems

Social theories that build on the notion of "system," from Parsons to Luhmann, have the great merit to capture a major feature of human societies: the human tendency to systematize linkages between entities in order to elaborate consistent and auto-referenced worlds. But these theories frequently overlook the cognitive and material operations which achieve systematic linkages. The analyst's task should not be limited to the identification of a "medium," such as money or influence (Parsons), which is supposed to shape human relationships and codify them. The comparison shows that the first medium substantially differs from the second in that it is far more materialized. We need to explore in great detail the process of bringing consistency and establishing systematic linkages between entities through codification or, more generally, what I analyzed as "investments of forms." (Thevenot, 1984) What does this systematization specifically demand, by comparison with other ways of engaging reality in non-codified forms? Answers to this question cannot be found within the systemic approach. Habermas was quite aware of this problem when he elaborated his theory of communicative action to dispose of an external support and be able to criticize the intrusion of systemic relations into politics. I propose another avenue of research. While I fully acknowledge the role played by systematic integration, I do not stay at the level of codified knowledge and behaviour. My contention is that issues of justice and deliberation on the good and its realization cannot develop without the prior constitution of systematic linkages between human beings and their natural or artefactual environment. And these issues cannot be reduced to codification.

A Relevant Reality for the Good

The systematic generalization of a certain way human beings capture their environment is an historical process. But it also depends on the potential capacities which the human body, nature or human artifices can offer. They allow for a certain systematic generalization of the commerce between human beings and their milieu. Such an extension is not only a "social construction" or an ideological elaboration. The present constitution of a new kind of systematic linkage in terms of "information" illustrates both the material and ideological aspects of the process. First comes the development of a whole range of techniques which enhances human communicative abilities. The construction of effective communicative systems is a prerequisite for the comparison of "informational" capacities. Such comparisons pave the way to a questioning of the kind of good which such capacities involve, and of the forms of injustice in their actual distribution.

Acknowledging a certain type of systemic relationship between human beings and their milieu is not enough to expose a new polity. Allegedly factual statements about an "information society" actually encompass and conceal assumptions about the good. A democratic debate demands that they be explicitly stated. It requires the constitution of a new political and moral grammar. Thus, the mixed material and ideological crafting of a new system of relationship makes forth to the delineation of a new kind of common good which would support a generalized "information worth." The canonical distinction between facts and values hinders the proper understanding of the joint constitution of a new systematic form of realism articulated with a new specification of the common good. The value/fact distinction dangerously places politics in the alternative of either a powerless idealism or an amoral realism.

The elaboration of the general forms of evaluation that are needed for an "equipped" humanity can be sketched in the following way. A certain way of systematically relating human beings to their non-human environment makes comparable the human capacities which are enabled by this mode of relation. The comparison of situations where these capacities are involved leads to the assessment of unequal capacities, and creates a tension with a fundamental moral orientation towards an equal human dignity. Questioning this inequality brings forward issues of injustice and considerations on the good. Modern societies elaborated general forms of value or, more precisely, of evaluation and judgment, in order to deal with this tension. They offer most legitimate frames for disputes which refer to the horizon of the public. In *De la justification* Boltanski and I singled out six "orders of worth" in terms of *inspired, domestic* (or trustworthiness), *opinion, civic, market* and *industrial* worth. (see table 1) (Boltanski and Thévenot, 1991) Each of them integrates a part of the *furnishing* of societies within a common humanity through the specification of the common good. We analyzed these orders and their common grammar. To provide a simplified presentation of this grammar, I shall mention that unequal capacities constitute an order of worth on the following two types of conditions:

(1) The inequality of states of worth has to be related to the characterization of a common good: the most worthy states should be shown to be beneficial to the least worthy.

(2) A state of worth should not be attached permanently to a human being, because of the risk of creating a stable differentiation which would challenge the idea of common humanity and equal dignity. Worthiness is not a status, but evolves in relation to an effective capacity which has to be put to a test with regards to a relevant reality.

Making the Reality and the Good More General

Putting the grammar of the most legitimate "orders of worth" in the perspective of our present debate, I shall contend that this grammar introduces the possibility of a joint enlargement:

(1) Of the format of the relevant reality which supports the evaluation. Entities qualify for a worth assessment as far as they take place in a generalized systematic relationship between human beings and their environment. Entities qualify as market good, technical implement, sign, patrimony, etc. Depending on these qualifications, the relevant information has different formats: price, statistical measure, oral and exemplary report, semiotic representation, etc.

(2) Of the format of the good which governs the evaluation. Orders of worth result from the aggrandizement of values up to the scope of a common good compatible with a common humanity.

In *De la justification* we have drawn both on empirical studies on practices of justifications and criticisms performed in everyday situations, and on a series of Western political philosophers each of whom systematically developed one of these notions of worth. These orders of worth are clearly historical and cultural constructions. Some of them are less and less

Table 1 ORDERS OF WORTH

	Market	Industrial	Domestic	Opinion	Civic	Inspired
Mode of evaluation (worth)	Price	Productivity, efficiency	Esteem, reputation, trustworthi- ness	Renown interest	Collective creativeness	Innovation,
Format of relevant information	Monetary	Measurable: criteria, statistics	Oral, exemplary, anecdote	Semiotic official	Formal,	Emotional
Qualified objects	Market goods and	Technical objects, methods services	Patrimony specific asset	Sign, media	Rule	Emotionally invested body or object: artists, religious
Elementary relation	Exchange	Functional link	Trust	Recognition	Solidarity	Passion
Human qualification	Desire, purchasing power	Professional competency, expertise	Authority	Celebrity	Equality	Creativity, ingenuity
Time formation	Short-term, flexibility	Long-term planned future	Customary path	Vogue, trend	Perennial	Rupture, revolution
Space formation	Global marketplace	Homogeneous, Cartesian space	Anchoring in proximity	Communica- tion network	Detachment	Perennial

able to ground people's justifications whereas other ones are emerging. I mentioned the current elaboration of an "information worth" and also studied the emergence of a new "green worth." (Thévenot, Moody and Lafaye, 2000)

What can I say of this historical and cultural process of emergence in the perspective of this Congress? The empirical and philosophical material which served to analyze these orders of worth came from European culture. But I am concerned to test the validity of the analytical framework in other cultural areas. The work was done in a comparison with the United States, and I intend to extend this comparative perspective to a larger range of cultures. A rationale for such a comparative investigation comes from the fact that orders of worth were built from an effort to overcome a great diversity of more "cultural" values. Coordination with the anonymous alien raises the need to cope with an extended notion of humanity, and to surmount value discrepancies and obtain shared forms of evaluations. I shall here insist on the way each order of worth results from an attempt to generalize to a common humanity a set of values that have been currently used, in much more specific and contextual terms, to coordinate conducts in more limited cultural and historical domains.

Orders of Worth:
The Ground for a Critical and Realist Pluralism

The "Market Worth" of Competition

The construction of a *market worth* requires two types of expansion of the various kinds of exchange relationship which human societies have developed:

(1) A generalized formatting of the merchandises and human agents involved in the relationship of commercial exchange. By contrast to many traditional forms of personal or gift relationship, a generalized market common good requires the detachment from personal ties, an anonymous and common identity of people and things, and a perfect transferability of ownership. People are principally qualified for the market by their desire to purchase commodities.

(2) A generalized common good which offers a unified principle for commercial exchange: market competition. Price is clearly the

measurable appraisal which corresponds to this common good of market competition.

The sphere of economic relations is not uniquely governed by market worth. Economic actions are based on, at least, two main forms of coordination. One is *market* competition, another is the *industrial* order of technical efficiency and productivity, each of them supporting a different kind of reality test. They also sustain different formation of time. While the market competition test is particularly short-term, the industrial test relies on long-term investments.

The "Industrial Worth" of Efficiency and Productivity

All human societies developed tools and techniques. The construction of an *industrial worth* requires more in the two directions that I highlighted:

(1) A generalized formatting of things and people based on standardized and measurable technical capabilities instead of personalized or localized skills and craftsmanship. The most qualified persons are experts. The words used to describe their functional qualities can also be used to qualify things. They are said to be worthy when they are efficient, productive, operational. They implement tools, methods, criteria, plans, figures, etc.

(2) A generalized common good characterized in terms of technical efficiency. The *industrial* worth can be measured on a scale of professional capabilities.

Connected to the production of material goods, industrial worth is upheld by way of organizational devices directed towards future planning and investment. The technical objects which qualify for this industrial worth are those which contribute to the formation of a future-oriented notion of time and a Cartesian notion of space and topography.

The "Domestic Worth" of Trustworthiness

Trying to expand personal relationship into a more stable and transportable kind of mutual link is a very common effort among human societies. This process is at the very basis of what we usually call a shared "culture." It leads to placing greater value on things and people which are viewed as more acquainted and proximate. Boltanski and I identified as the *domestic* worth of trustworthiness a construction which aims at a most general extension of these personalized and anchored bonds and valuations. This construction assumes:

(1) A generalized formatting of people and things transforming them into grounds which guarantee a generalized trust and confidence. *Domestic* worth depends on a hierarchy of trust based on a chain of personal dependencies. To qualify for this worth, the person is related to his/her belonging, to a family, a lineage, a patrimony. Customary skills and crafts which are disqualified with regard to the *industrial* worth are, by contrast, highly valued as patrimony and heritage within this *domestic* worth.

(2) In order to obtain a transportable judgment of trustworthiness which might be valid for a whole common humanity and not a particular network, one should overcome the specific distinctiveness of cultures and build a common good. This is achieved on the basis of the comparable process through which patrimony, heritage, legacy and tradition are made valuable in diverse cultures.

Heritage supports a notion of time which places value on memory and which is past-oriented. This does not prevent the dynamics of constant re-interpretation of the past from the view of the present situation. The formation of space is also quite different from an homogeneous Cartesian space since spaces extend from an anchoring in proximity.

The "Worth of Renown" of Opinion

If, in a *domestic* world, worth has value only in a hierarchical chain of beings, worth is nothing but the result of other people's opinion in the world of *renown*. Again, societies developed many political configurations which are based on fame and visibility. Court societies offer clear examples of such configurations. The extension of a worth of renown in the opinion requires:

(1) The formatting and measurement of people's worth on the basis of conventional signs of public notoriety. Qualified persons are well-known personalities, movie stars, opinion leaders, journalists. They are worthy and great when they are famous, recognized, successful, or convincing among public opinion. The current objects in this world are trademarks, badges, logos, message transmitters and receivers, press releases and booklets.

(2) The common good is a generalized celebrity which strongly
     supports a mode of coordination based on conventional signs of
     recognition. Worthiness rises with the number of individuals who
     grant their recognition. It is hence entirely unrelated to the realm
     of personal dependencies.

This order of worth sustains the formation of a highly volatile time,
unfolding in vogues or trends. Communication media takes the space of
recognition to be planetary instead of limited to a restricted space of
visibility.

The "Civic Worth" of Rules Enforcing Equality and Solidarity

Mutual reciprocity which regulates personal relationships can be generalized by an order of worth which strongly departs from the *domestic*
gradient of proximity and hierarchy of esteem. While aiming at solidarity,
the *civic* worth involves, in an opposite direction, the most complete detachment from personal dependency. The generalization goes the following
way:

(1) People and things are formatted in a formal shape which dis-
     connects them from any local or personalized attachment.
     Worthy people are representative of a collective person. Impor-
     tant persons are, therefore, federations, public communities,
     representatives or delegates. The relevant objects are highly
     codified, such as rules and procedures. Praiseworthy relation-
     ships are those which involve or mobilize people for a collective
     action.
(2) The common good is oriented towards equality and achieved
     through solidarity. Persons are less worthy if seen as particulars,
     following the dictates of a selfish will, and, in contrast, worthy if
     seen as members of the disembodied sovereign, exclusively
     concerned with the general interest.

Civic time is perennial although rules are to be changed by the
collective will. Civic space is highly universalized, but this extension
faces the contradiction of solidarity mechanisms which are commonly
bounded to institutionalized groups or nations.

The "Inspired Worth" of Creativeness

Although emotions are deeply entrenched in bodily expressions, they support modes of coordination among human societies. In various and separated domains such as religion, aesthetics or even technical innovation, human beings place common value on deep moves which bring about disruption among everyday routine. The worth of *inspiration* offers the possibility to cross the boundaries of these domains and refer to a generalized form of evaluation and coordination.

(1) People and things qualify for this order of worth inasmuch as their singularities express creativeness. Inspired worth arises, particularly, in the personal body when prepared by asceticism, and especially through emotions. Its expressions are diverse and many-sided: holiness, creativity, artistic sensibility, imagination etc. The qualified beings are, for example, spirits, crazy people, artists, children. These beings are worthy when they are odd, wonderful, emotional. Their typical way of acting is to dream, to imagine, to rebel, or to have living experiences.

(2) The common good rests on the idea that inspiration and creativity benefit everyone, and that people can commonly assess this kind of worth in spite of the singularity of the traits and events that are seen as valuable.

Conclusion

The Variety of Scope and Worth of the Goods to Be Critically Confronted in a Global Coordination

The moral strength of political liberalism originates in its ability to take pluralism into account and to offer some procedure of integration of this plurality. Another appeal of this model comes from its support of the notion of individualized agency. As a result of these two main features, the public is viewed in this liberal perspective as the composition of the kind of individual goods or interests which govern the conducts of individual agents. The composition of such goods in procedures of negotiation is commonly viewed as the core mechanism of the diverse regulatory bodies which develop all over the world.

But this model should not obscure other modes of composition of the public which are based on the aggrandizement of goods into orders of

worth. They advantageously integrate within the polity a variety of relations to the material environment, without confining this environment to
the state of market goods. While being compatible with a common set of
requirements oriented towards universalization with regard to a common
humanity, the different orders of worth offer a plurality of legitimate forms
of evaluation which allows for a dynamical process of critique and
justification. These repertoires of evaluation sustain the process of a global
expansion in human relationships while maintaining critical differences.
Each order of worth constitutes the basis for the radical criticism of the
others. This *critical* relationship between the different orders of worth
allows in particular to question some undue extensions of the market
worth. The organization of evaluative pluralism also requires *compromises*
between these generalized goods and not only between individualized
ones. It may sustain a critical pluralism because of the way things are
realistically involved. The plurality of worths initiates dynamics of
criticism, justification and compromise which go beyond the value- or
culture-relativism, while escaping a fierce confrontation of entrenched
values shared by particular communities. But we should also bear in mind
the reductions which threaten the extension of each order of worth: the
limitation to a bounded community; the reduction to systemic constraints
of reality (ignoring the dimension of the good); inversely, the restriction to
ideas (ignoring the realistic dimension of the human commerce with
things).

A French-American comparison of the way people produce public
judgments on people and things (Lamont and Thévenot, 2000; Moody and
Thévenot, 2000; Thévenot and Lamont, 2000), demonstrated that both
models are actually enforced in procedures of composition of the public
good in the United States, although the weight of the different orders of
worth and the kind of compromises strongly differ from France. The liberal
language of multiple interests, even with its extension to multiculturalism,
does not fully capture the variety of scope and of worth of the goods which
are confronted in the procedures of composition.

While this talk deliberately focused on the aggrandizement of values
needed for large-scope coordination, I don't want to suggest that generalized forms of evaluation are to replace other forms based on more
localized kinds of good. I shall illustrate this point in conclusion with the
very hot issue coined in France by the term *exception culturelle*, and which
is not a specifically French problem. The question is the following. Should
we conceive and treat "cultural goods" as any other market goods and

make sure that the rules of free market competition regulate their distribution? In the light of what I have presented in this talk, my answer is no. We should rather make sure that debates and decision making within globalized regulatory agencies do not only preserve a diversity of cultural identities but also a diversity of orders of worth in addition to *market* competition, amongst which are certainly what I presented as *domestic* and *inspired* orders of worth.

Notes

1. For an introduction to this line of argument in English, see Boltanski and Thévenot, 1999, 2000; for a short presentation and positioning of the research programme, see Thévenot, 1995. For an analysis of economical organizations as devices for compromising complexity, see Thévenot, 2001c. For discussions in English of this research programme, see Dodier, 1999 and Wagner, 1994; on its more recent extensions, see Wagner 1999; for a comparison with Callon's and Latour's framework and a contrast with Bourdieu's, see Bénatouïl, 1999; on the implication for economic theory, see Wilkinson, 1997.

2. "To live together in the world means essentially that a world of things is between those who have it in common, as a table is located between those who sit around it; the world, like every in-between, relates and separates men at the same time. The public realm, as the common world, gathers us together and yet prevents our falling over each other, so to speak. What makes mass society so difficult to bear is not the number of people involved, or at least not primarily, but the fact that the world between them has lost its power to gather them together, to relate and to separate them. The weirdness of this situation resembles a spiritualistic séance where a number of people gathered around a table might suddenly, through some magic trick, see the table vanish from their midst, so that two persons sitting opposite each other were no longer separated but also would be entirely unrelated to each other by anything tangible." (Arendt, 1958: 52–53)

References

Arendt, Hannah (1958). *The Human Condition*. Chicago: Chicago University Press.

Bénatouïl, Thomas (1999). "A Tale of Two Sociologies." *European Journal of Social Theory*, Vol. 2, No. 3, August, pp. 379–96.

Boltanski, Luc, and Laurent Thévenot (1991). *De la justification. Les économies de la grandeur*. Paris: Gallimard.

Boltanski, Luc, and Laurent Thévenot (1999). "The Sociology of Critical Capacity." *European Journal of Social Theory*, Vol. 2, No. 3, August, pp. 359–77.

Boltanski, Luc, and Laurent Thévenot (2000). "The Reality of Moral Expectations: A Sociology of Situated Judgment." (Translated by Jo Smets). *Philosophical Explorations*, Vol. 3, No. 3, pp. 208–31.

Dodier, Nicolas (1993). "Action as a Combination of Common Worlds." *The Sociological Review*, Vol. 41, No. 3, pp. 556–71.

Lamont, Michele, and Laurent Thévenot, eds. (2000). *Rethinking Comparative Cultural Sociology: Repertoires of Evaluation in France and the United States.* Cambridge: Cambridge University Press.

Moody, Michael, and Laurent Thévenot (2000). "Comparing Models of Strategy, Interests, and the Public Good in French and American Environmental Disputes." Lamont Michèle and Laurent Thévenot, eds., *Rethinking Comparative Cultural Sociology: Repertoires of Evaluation in France and the United States*. Cambridge: Cambridge University Press, pp. 273–306.

Thévenot, Laurent (1984). "Rules and Implements: Investment in Forms." *Social Science Information*, Vol. 23, No. 1, pp. 1–45.

——— (1990). "L'action qui convient." Patrick Pharo and L. Quéré, eds., *Les formes de l'action*. Paris: Ed. de l'EHESS (Raisons pratiques 1), pp. 39–69.

——— (1995). "New Trends in French Social Sciences." *Culture*, Vol. 9, No. 2, pp. 1–7.

——— (2001a). "Pragmatic Regimes Governing the Engagement With the World." Karen Knorr-Cetina, Theodore Schatzki and Eike von Savigny, eds., *The Practice Turn in Contemporary Theory*. London: Routledge, pp. 56–73.

——— (2001b). "Which Road to Follow? The Moral Complexity of an 'Equipped' Humanity." John Law and Annemarie Mol, eds., *Complexities in Science, Technology and Medicine*. Durham, North Carolina: Duke University Press (forthcoming).

——— (2001c). "Organized Complexity: Conventions of Coordination and the Composition of Economic Arrangements." *European Journal of Social Theory*, Vol. 4, No. 4, pp. 405–25.

Thévenot, Laurent, and Michele Lamont (2000). "Exploring the French and American Polity." Michele Lamont and Laurent Thévenot, eds., *Rethinking Comparative Cultural Sociology: Repertoires of Evaluation in France and the United States*. Cambridge: Cambridge University Press, pp. 307–27.

Thévenot, Laurent, Michael Moody, and Claudette Lafaye (2000). "Forms of Valuing Nature: Arguments and Modes of Justification in Environmental Disputes." Michele Lamont and Laurent Thévenot, eds., *Rethinking Comparative Cultural Sociology: Repertoires of Evaluation in France and the United States*. Cambridge: Cambridge University Press, pp. 229–72.

Wagner, Peter (1994). "Action, Coordination, and Institution in Recent French Debates." *The Journal of Political Philosophy*, Vol. 2, No. 3, pp. 270–89.

Wilkinson, John (1997). "A New Paradigm for Economic Analysis?" *Economy and Society*, Vol. 26, No. 3, August, pp. 305–39.

The Media and the Dispersion of Knowledge

Marc Ferro

Professor Thévenot has raised issues concerning new kinds of pluralism, and I will deal with old and new kinds of knowledge, a global approach which fits in with what we have been discussing at this Congress. As discussed elsewhere, the multiplicity of media today creates new difficulties because each medium — newspapers, cinema, television — produces different elements of knowledge, and these elements are not at all connected. For instance, during the different stages of our high school education, or at the university level, we study distinct disciplines, history, economics, literature and so on. Indeed, they are already disconnected. For example, if you are a British citizen, studying foreign languages, say French, you will never have to read anything about Goethe, Cervantes, or Dostoevsky. Worse, in France, you can read in literature that the French Philosopher Jean Jacques Rousseau prepared a political constitution for Corsica, during the 1760s. But the traditional history of France doesn't tell you that Corsica had a republican constitution before the French revolution. Later, at the university level, each discipline is apt to divide itself in many sub-disciplines, each trying to dominate the others.

I used to call this phenomenon, a specific kind of imperialism, the sectorial imperialism of each social science. Each one in turn — linguistics, demography, anthropology and so on, is trying now to explain all the problems and integrate them inside the system of its own rules. This also happens when we pick up the newspaper. When reading one, the organization of information is completely different. For this conference, I checked some foreign newspapers last week, *El Pais* in Spain, *Frankfurter Allgemeine Zeitung* in Germany, *Le Monde* in France, *Il Corriera della Sera* in Italy and the *New York Times* in America. You can easily check that the front page is more or less the same everywhere. Last week it was occupied by the same event, the tragedy of the Indian Airlines crash and so on.

But the main point is the constant organization of the table of contents. It is the reproduction either of the organization of powers, or of the different activities of society. Usually its organization is comparable to the different departments of a government — foreign affairs, home affairs, war office, health department and so on. For instance, in *El Pais*, you have justice, culture, sport, and a special thick section on finance. It is the same in German newspapers with some specific pages on art and social problems, and a thick section on careers. Naturally, there is no connection between these sections. Neither are the lectures of scholars in the universities connected with this news. I have tried doing this many times when I was a professor with little success. From time to time there is a link between the leading article and the others, but often when you read a historical article in a newspaper, in the case of a commemoration, this article remains in the past, not connected with the events that have happened since, as if the past was dead forever.

Next we should look at a field, for example, television programs. The striking point is the bureaucratic organization of a channel, news, magazine, fiction, cartoons, documentaries and so on. Each department is completely disconnected from the others. Last week the news told us that the new Russian president Vladimir Putin spent his new year in Chechnya, the magazine told us Putin's past in Germany in the KBG, and later his association with Sobchak, the Mayor of St. Petersburg. The news gives you scoops, but no explanations, no analysis, while the magazines give you analysis, explanations, but no news. However there *are* some connections between television programs and newspapers. In France, for instance, reading *Le Monde,* the main afternoon newspaper at four o'clock, you can check that the television news at eight o'clock is more or less a repeat of what you could have read some hours before. On the contrary, newspapers do not like to borrow their images from television. Television journalists are reading the newspapers, while their compatriots are not watching television. What we see here is a professional rivalry between different media. Each medium gives us different information or the same information from different points of view, with or without images. The question is: how can both relationships or interconnections be seen in the context of such dispassionate information? My feeling is that we have to reverse our point of view, and instead of approaching the problem seen by us as readers or onlookers, as an audience, we have to reconsider it as if we were producers of knowledge, which perhaps we are.

For one generation, especially since the end of communism in Russia, the Western world has successfully debated the nature and function of history as a discipline. Not to explore only the past, but to explore past and present and the connection between past and present. This study also involves the nature of newsreels and fiction films. This debate is a result of several phenomena. The first phenomenon is the duplication or mul-tiplication of the forms of history, which is seen in films, television programs, novels, and cartoon strips. This has relativized the traditional discussion of history which was previously the domain of schools and scholars alone. In the consciousness of today's society, there is a certain telescoping of historical knowledge, with the verdict emanating from these various sources.

Second, the changes that the world has seen, especially de-colonization, have had the effect of multiplying the various centres of historical production. Besides white history which itself varies according to ideology, other perceptions and interpretations have emerged which are not Eurocentric, for example that which have come from the Islamic and Arab world, from Japan and other places. Parallel to this and in contrast to the nation state vision of the past, many societies have claimed their right to a place in history — Blacks in the United States, Basque and Bretons in France for example. The idea that there may be a single or universal acceptable version of history has simply become an illusion. The bank-ruptcy of ideology has had the effect of making historical discourses less authoritative. Such questioning affects not only the interpretation of such events, for instance, the inevitability or not of the October Revolution, but also the very choice of facts to be discussed and regarded as significant. Is it more important to study wars or taxation during the reign of Queen Victoria?

The questioning and relativization of historical discourse have become all the more confusing because historians themselves have for many years have been attacking traditional and chronological history. The narration of history must be deconstructed and used as a starting point not as an end for historical analysis. Narrative has become a stage in analysis. Besides, it has become clear that the division of history into chronological parts, so very useful for the reconstruction for what had been experienced, nonetheless ignores long-term historical processes such as social and economic trends, revolution in families and beliefs and so on. Furthermore, some scholars have become conscious of this kind of problem and have been struck by the fact that people want to understand the connection between the present and the past, without any effort to make comprehensible the origins of our

times. With this view of history, newsreels and the cinema would lose all
their significance. Here I would like to give a global and schematic analysis
of all the main approaches of history and politics.

Now our problem is how to approach this connection between history
and news, between academic scholarship, professional journalism, and
fiction filmmakers, discretion implying for us that history is not only
knowledge of the past, of ancient times, but the relationship between past
and present and the analysis of continuities and ruptures. But first we have
to consider the global approaches followed by historians, social scientists
and others.

The first approach will be the philosophical or political one, that gives
the meaning of the evidence — history's progress, history's decay and so
on. This approach has dominated till now, either from a Christian view-
point of history or a Marxist one.

In the second approach, the scholar tries to collect data and other
information to organize a chronological representation of the past, a general history of that country or of the world, a general and encyclopaedic
approach that is often Eurocentric.

The third approach is an experimental one. It doesn't accept any
teleological vision of history, but tries to ask specific questions and then
attempts to solve them. If I dare use an analogy and say that experimental
history is similar to experimental medicine in the sense that ancient
medicine and traditional history were both trying to analyze global problems that have to do with life and death and the meaning of history. On the
contrary, modern medicine endeavours to classify different diseases in the
same way that this kind of history tries to classify the different kinds of
problems, for example that of prices and salary, taxes and strikes, and race
and class. The new historians are asking questions and trying to give
answers.

I have said that there are three approaches, but usually these three
approaches are mixed, and the secret of a historian — the art, is in this
mixture. But if you are a good reader you can perhaps see that often they
do not know what they are doing. Take for instance Fernand Braudel in
France. His *Mediterraneé*, a global compendium of all the problems of the
Mediterranean, is considered the epitome of the third approach. The information presented in this book is gorgeous, splendid and professional.
This third kind of book is supposed to be free of any teleological view as
indeed it is. Nevertheless Braudel tells us in his conclusion that the influence of people *on* their history is nothing as compared with the permanent

influence of situations, traditions, geography and so *on* the people. That means that he is a determinist historian but not a Marxist one.

In Marxist historiography, some people are in the wave of history, some people are not in the wave of history, some are useful, some are useless, and history is apt to become a kind of technical code if not a moral code. I have mentioned that historiography is often a mixture of these three approaches, but during the nineteenth century, the first and the second approaches married and this established history expelled from the field the experimental approach, so much so that the forerunners of experimental history were not considered historians, but as writers. Take for instance, Montesquieu, Taine, and some sociologists, like Durkheim, or Weber. They were not exactly historians because they didn't study the past, in the sense that they did not study the evolution of societies but a specific moment, a specific problem, a specific aspect, of the histories of societies. But Durkheim studying suicide was a follower of Claude Bernard, a physician, and one of the real fathers of the Annals School even if Bloch, Febvre and others liked better to be linked with geography than with sociology because the link with geography was nearest with the natural and experimental sciences.

Therefore during the nineteenth and twentieth centuries the third approach was half eliminated and the victory of political history mixed with ideology was such a complete one that now history is identified with it. This was in reality a kind of history stemming from institutions and for the glory of state, of church, the Communist Party in the Soviet Union, the Congress Party in India and so on. This kind of history used to be a commentary on the archives of the dominant institution expelling from the field information and news coming from elsewhere. It is a kind of history as seen by victorious people and organizations. This would be represented by a history of the United States as seen from the *wasp* point of view, or the story of colonization from an European point of view. Such a history is based on a hierarchy of sources. At its head, in all their glory, comes the words sealed by the great royal autograph and other holy texts whether Marxist or Maoist. Then comes the less important commentaries, laws, treaties, edicts of the Arab world, statistics, and at the end of the procession, like the humble third estate in black, come the private documents, anonymous witnesses whose role at most is to confirm the miraculous doings of the rulers. Such history from above is embodied in institutions. This is despite the fact that an anti-history that is also institutional may exist parallel to that of the victors whether they be church, party, nation or state. It could not of course have the same support, and sometimes survives in oral form or in films in countries where the people cannot write. If a written culture prevailed, it is a buried history.

The history of the defeated was first stated forcefully by colonial peoples, but it appears or reappears wherever a formally impotent social group feels threatened, exploited, degraded, and its identity banished from history. It then revives its own traditions. Quebecois in Canada, Chicanos in the United States, Berbers in Algeria, The League of Women and all the other outcasts have resurrected their daily lives and actions of the past. Or perhaps a parallel history can be constructed. One of the most phenomenal characteristics of institutional anti-history, is that it looks to its own communities out of its own borders, and defines itself in terms of others whether centres of power beliefs or nations or whatever.

Next to experimental and official or traditional history, societies' memories, whether individual or collective, are other centres of production of history. Sometimes and in some particular places this centre can be confused with anti-history, when the group can only preserve its identity through traditions whether oral or cultural. However this kind of history is different because it doesn't have specialist servants at its beck and call — that is, professional historians. Hence, it doesn't have to preserve the rules of the guild. A signatory of this kind of history is that it is not subject to criticism. Another feature is that it often confuses time with myths and reality, especially as regards matters of origins.

History like this survives autonomous and intact and it has flourished despite all the denigration it may face in scholarly history, official or not. It is not transmitted in the same way as anti-history, but lives side-by-side with institutional history which it may have been itself in the distant past, so it has long vanished as such. In that case, it is not the historical content that changes with time. Rather, what changes are the attributes of history. Some of the Spanish festivals, such as *Moros y Christianos*, have remained unchanged since the sixteenth century which tell us the permanent vision of Christianity on Islam.

Naturally all films are a kind of social analysis, I mean documentary and fiction ones. But certainly at the present time, only newsreels and documentaries are considered documents by scholars. Fiction films and cinema are seen in relationship to the imaginary and not to knowledge. They are not seen as an expression of reality, but as a representation of it. Today, because the dogmas and customs of written tradition have been transposed to images, little trust is placed in the scientific testimony of fiction which appears similar to novels. Everyone knows that so-called serious people of science or politics have little faith in the novel or the imagination. They would rather trust statistics. Thus, by likening the film in some sense to writing, educated people tend to accept, if pressed, the testimony of documentary film but not the fiction film, and they don't accept is as a document or as a historical or social text. For them, the film works only with dreams as if dreams were not a part of reality. As if dreams and imagination were not one of the motives of human activity.

Now, I would like to compare the different modes of social analysis of these different kinds of history. Modes means to me here today, the choice of information, the principle of organization of history writing, the different forms of telling history, and some other aspects. The explicit function of each kind of history conceals the objectives of the participants and the creativity of each mode. The different kinds of history we are told are general history, anti-history, memory history, experimental history, fiction, newspapers, and newsreels.

First, the choice of information. The choice of information changes in each kind of history or rather the principle of selection changes. In traditional history and traditional texts in general history, there is a global preference, as I have already told you, for official documents coming from the leaders. So this kind of history is often a reproduction or critical reproduction of the vision of history of the establishment, or Nomenklatura. The information is residing in their own approach even if we criticize them. In this kind of history, and it is quite the same for anti-history, minor facts, two-line incidents are expelled from the field of the historians, because they are either local or without influence on global evolution. Murders for money, jealously, accidents, suicides, natural catastrophes can be eliminated because they are supposed to be without meaning. The catastrophe as a symptom of the impotence of power. Daily life is eliminated too because it doesn't change the global evolution of history. But long-term phenomenon are also absent. For instance, the history of the family, the history of anti-Semitism. The history of anti-Semitism is approached only when a crisis erupts.

In the case of historical memory, the principle of selection of information, is not a selection but an accumulation of information. Accumulation is the main aim of the historian so even a shoe discovered under a stone becomes a treasure. There is a kind of socialization of each document, not especially written archives as in general history. The specificity of the third kind of history, experimental history, in the choice of information, is obvious. Now, I am obliged to quote myself. For instance, in my first volume on the February 17 Revolution, I explained which information and documents I would use. I explained that I would use the first 300 telegrams sent by Russian citizens to the provisional government, and from the beginning I explained that this corpus would give me an idea of what the citizens hoped and desired, their aspirations and that later I would compare their demands with the social, economic and political programmes of the different political parties, so the reader could check what I was doing, why I was doing it and how I was doing it.

In a fiction film the organization of information is different. In the movie *Dr. Zhivago*, for example, the director chooses his information in connection with the problems that are interesting now — I mean when he was making his film, not the problems that were important during the actual revolution. For instance, we know that the bourgeois will be killed by the Bolsheviks, by Lenin, that is why the camera shows us Lenin and the Bolsheviks more than the anarchists or the socialist revolutionaries. Most filmmakers exhibit similar behaviour. I mean that when making a film, the producer wants to interest the audience and so chooses incidents of our time instead of ones of the past. In the February Revolution the anarchists were as important as the Bolsheviks, but it is hard to imagine that they existed when seeing *Dr. Zhivago*, because in 1956 the problem was Lenin and the connection between Stalinism and Leninism, not anarchism. On television newsreels and in newspapers, journalists are always chasing a scoop, and if possible an image, a striking image or event to catch the eye, but a striking image does not always contain important information.

The choice of information to be used is the first aspect. But in all kinds of history, it is the principal of how the information is organized that is different too.

For instance, in global and general history, it is the chronological that is the principle of organization, and a mistake in the dates is considered a crime. This is also the same in memory history. In experimental history, on the contrary, the principle of organization is not chronological, but logical, whether the analysis good or not. In historical fiction or film, the organization is based on the drama, in order to create suspense, despite the fact that the course of history does not follow an even tempo. History is not dramatically organized, nor there are pauses in history like in a novel or film. It is an illusion to believe that history and news can be seen as it actually happens. We can see some details but not the global overview.

Nevertheless television reporters show it as if it were a football competition. But this is just an illusion, because while we know the rules of a football match, we don't know the rules of a war. They are constantly changing. Nor is war is limited to recent events. Some decisions and actions related to the outbreak of war are subterranean and are not known till much later after the conclusion of hostilities. So, history doesn't obey the rules of tragedy, of melodrama, of sport.

The function and role of these kinds of history are different. For instance, the historical memory of my village, of the women, of the Armenians and so on, endeavours to reinforce their identity. History helps the group to be itself, to glorify its dignity. This kind of history, is often anonymous, like the Middle Ages. General and official history are apt to legitimize the official powers of king and country and this category of historians try to obtain honours and decorations. Practitioners in experimental history like to be considered as scholars and so thereby become a kind of intelligentsia and authority of their society.

As for the filmmakers, they are trying to give you pleasure and are motivated by their demand for beauty and their own narcissism. In television newsreels, the temptation of the journalist is to create events, not just to tell you what actually happened. What kind of improvement will there be in these different forms of history as science makes great strides? In the case of historical memory there is no creativity but only humility and pity. The creativity of new works on general history is rather in the new classification of facts that are selected by the historian. For instance, the new history of France by Burgiere and Reval in France show a very original and creative organization of facts. The creativity in experimental history can be seen in the choice of the plot and the stake of the film regarding their importance, quite the same as in a fiction film. But if the choice of situations and the stake of the story are well-defined, then a filmmaker can be the best historian in the world. For example *Potemkin*, even if the greater part of the information is untrue, the historical genius of Sergei Eisenstein is obvious.

These scattered observations and remarks were done to help you appreciate the how and whys of the stake of each element in a historical analysis with or without images. They also serve as keys to connect you with the knowledge that is coming towards you from all directions in a greater disorder everyday, and in a greater order in my paper.

Pluralism Without Relativism in Ethics

Gerard J. Hughes

For two and a half millennia, moral philosophy has been characterized, at least in the Western traditions, by two conflicting tendencies. On the one hand, there has been the conviction that the truths of ethics transcended the varieties of individual cultures and social conventions. Often it has been implicit in this tradition that if, in an ideal world, we all came to know the truth about ethics, we would all have the same moral beliefs; just as if, ideally, we all had a perfect understanding of physics or biochemistry, we would of course have reached the *same* understanding of those subjects. The moral world must have the same kind of unitary consistency as the world studied by the natural sciences. In their somewhat different ways, both Plato and Aristotle belong to this tradition, and contributed enormously to giving it a suitable theoretical backing.

On the other hand, there has been a recurring tendency for this position to be radically questioned. Especially at those periods in our history when people came into contact with cultures and civilizations which appeared to be very different from their own, and to have very different standards of ethical behaviour, it occurred to many philosophers to suggest that morality is based on nothing more than human conventions — the various ways in which the members of different societies had come to agree to live together. This reaction to intercultural contact characterized the century before Plato, as it has characterized the century which concluded the last millennium. This view has been reinforced by a growing conviction that the tradition is wrong, because it is quite misleading to see a parallel between the ideal state of the physical sciences and the ideal state of moral knowledge. The more we find out about the physical sciences the more we shall find ourselves in agreement: but there is no reason to suppose that the same is true of ethics. Indeed, we should perhaps abandon altogether the picture of a single moral world, parallel to the physical world in which we all live, whose characteristics we are all intent upon discovering.

In this paper, I would like to offer some reflections on these recurrent tendencies in moral philosophy. In particular, I shall argue that we do not have to decide between just two polar alternatives. Between the view that there is one ideally correct set of moral beliefs for everyone, and the view that morality is so bound up with a particular culture and its history that there is no reason to suppose that it will be the same from one culture to another, there is the view for which I shall argue: that morality is indeed pluralist, but not relativist.

Some Definitions

Relativism

The dispute between relativists and absolutists in ethics is a serious and long-standing dispute. Unfortunately, however, the two terms have also been used to refer to a confusing variety of different issues, which I need to clear out of the way before tackling the central problem. It is most important to use the term to identify a philosophical position which is both genuinely different from moral absolutism, and at the same time offers an alternative view which must be taken seriously.

It is not controversial that there are at least some differences between the moralities of different cultures. What is controversial is the interpretation to be put upon such differences. An absolutist will say that such differences are best accounted for by supposing that at least one of the conflicting positions is mistaken. Differences in moral beliefs are not evidence for relativism in ethics any more than differences of belief about the causes of schizophrenia are evidence for relativism in medicine. The moral relativist, on the other hand, wishes to insist that the explanation for such differences has to go much deeper. Either way, though, that there are such differences is common ground between relativist and absolutist.

Secondly, it is not a matter of serious controversy that different circumstances will make different moral demands upon people. Parents have some duties towards their children which other people do not have towards those same children Those who are sick have claims upon us which those who are healthy do not. Of course it is often a matter of dispute *which* circumstances make a morally significant difference and which do not. Thus it is a matter of dispute when, if at all, the fact that someone is male rather than female should make a difference to how they should be treated. But such disputes can easily be disputes between two moral absolutists; indeed, differences of opinion between moral absolutists typically have to do with precisely this kind of question. It is extremely important to recognize that moral absolutists do not need to, and usually do not, believe that moral principles are exceptionless or inflexible. The moral truth to which absolutists aspire may well be complex, not simple.

Thirdly, I take it as beyond dispute that everyone should guide their actions according to their own sincere moral beliefs. I should be ready to praise people for following their own conscientious opinions, even when I disagree with those opinions and would try to persuade them that their opinions might be mistaken. Indeed, it is the relativist who might find it harder consistently to accept this kind of statement; since to say that everyone ought to follow their conscientious beliefs itself seems to be an absolutist moral claim rather than a relativist one. As Plato famously argued, the relativist needs to answer the question whether they think that their relativist position is only relatively true — true only for those who are relativist — or whether it is absolutely true. I do not here wish to go into the details of this debate; it is sufficient for my present purpose to show that absolutists can easily defend freedom of conscience; perhaps more easily than relativists. At any rate, relativists must do more than claim that people ought to act as they sincerely believe they should act.

Fourthly, there are philosophers and others who would claim that there is no question of truth or falsity in ethics at all; that what are called "value judgments" do not make truth claims, but rather express decisions or emotional commitments. I shall not argue against these views here: suffice it to say that both relativists and absolutists are agreed that it is proper to speak of truth in ethics: where they disagree is in how moral truth is to be characterized.

So much for the preliminary ground-clearing. Relativism is a philosophical view which is quite distinct from anything I have so far said. The central core of relativism is a thesis about non-comparability. The relativist claims that there is no morally neutral basis for comparing or assessing different moralities. Nobody can ever be in a position to say that one moral outlook is better or worse than another, or that it corresponds more closely to the moral facts, or that it contains more or less moral truth.

Pluralism

Like "relativism," the term "pluralism" is not always used in exactly the same way by different writers. I shall later distinguish three different ways in which pluralism might be thought to arise in the context of ethics. But in general, an ethical pluralist will claim that there can be several incompatible moral views all of which can be equally defended. For the moment, I wish simply to state that I shall be arguing that relativism in ethics is a mistaken view: but that pluralism in ethics is in all likelihood a correct view.

To many absolutists and to many relativists alike, this intermediate position of mine will seem to be the worst of both worlds. The relativist will criticize me for trying to embrace absolutist views in a half-hearted way instead of recognizing that once one has accepted pluralism one has to accept a full-fledged relativism. On the other hand, absolutists will urge that the only coherent version of absolutism is the view that there is just one ideally correct view of morality, and that to deny this is in the end to abandon absolutism altogether. Both criticisms depend on the view that pluralism entails relativism; they differ only in the conclusion they draw from this: for the absolutist, that entailment constitutes a *reductio ad absurdum* of the pluralist position; for the relativist it might seem to be a good argument in his favour.

The Arguments for Relativism, and Their Limits

Many of the arguments for relativism fail because they establish positions that no absolutist would be concerned to deny, but which are mistakenly thought to be relativist. I shall consider a few of these arguments now only to reject them completely. But this consideration will pave the way for what I take to be a more serious argument for a genuinely relativist conclusion.

I have already pointed out that no absolutist in his or her senses ever wished to hold the preposterous view that circumstances never make a difference to what a person should do. However, and perhaps more plausibly, it has seemed to many people that no absolutist could admit that the mere fact of living in a different culture might in itself be a morally significant circumstance which would make a difference to how one should behave. If that is accepted, then how one ought to behave will depend on the culture in which one lives. So we are invited to think of the many influences which have contributed to the formation of different cultures: differences in climate, in economic resources, in technological development.

Responding to these changes, different cultures have developed different systems of property and ownership, different patterns of family relationships and inheritance, different styles of relaxation, decision-making, and government. Surely, it is argued, these factors are of crucial importance for how people should live: and since these factors are relative to different cultures, that conclusion is relativist.

There are several possible responses to this argument. The most extreme kind of absolutist might try to insist that any individual should behave in precisely the same way no matter which society that individual inhabits. But surely this version of absolutism is highly implausible, if only because it would on occasions at least require that people do the impossible. It makes sense to speak of moral duties, obligations and virtues only when it is possible, in the circumstances, to perform those duties and develop those virtues. In default of the economic and technological resources, or in a very alien social environment, many actions and policies will prove to be simply impossible to carry out.

A somewhat more cautious reaction on the part of some absolutists might be to say that, while it is true that in circumstances where the climate is very difficult, or economic resources very limited, or technology very under-developed, morality might well require one to behave differently from the way one would behave in a more affluent or developed society. Still, this is a far cry from the ideal situation, and not a good model for ethics. Ideally speaking, then, there is just one way in which everyone should behave. But this argument conceals a confusion. Of course if by developing new technologies or new resources it is possible to provide much better opportunities for individual and social development, then every effort should be made to do so. I would add only that such improvements are perhaps unlikely to be unambiguously better in all respects, so one should be hesitant before concluding that they will clearly be better overall. But suppose that no such opportunities for such development present themselves. It is still one thing to say that in difficult and less than ideal circumstances one will be faced with many uncomfortable decisions, it is quite another thing to suggest that the decisions one has to take in such circumstances must somehow be morally inadequate. They might well be exactly what the circumstances require. A sensible version of absolutism cannot require us to live as if we never had to face difficult choices. I conclude then that it is obviously true that in different cultural circumstances we will often have to make different moral decisions, if only for the reasons I have given. This is a conclusion that no sensible absolutist would deny.

So I believe, as I have already suggested, that the best reply to the argument from the diversity of cultural requirements is to deny that the conclusion is relativist in any important sense. To accept that in different circumstances people might have to behave differently is not in itself a relativist conclusion at all. It *would be* relativist were it combined with the claim that there is no way in which one can neutrally assess the demands which a particular culture places on its members. But the mere fact of cultural variation does not even begin to provide an argument for that conclusion.

An altogether different type of argument has sometimes been used to support relativism. It is argued that moral tolerance is a virtue, that relativists are committed to commending tolerance, whereas absolutists are committed to rejecting tolerance as a virtue altogether. Indeed it is sometimes supposed that absolutists must inevitably *impose* their moral beliefs upon others. On the contrary, though, I suggest that there are good reasons to suppose that the opposite is the case. If two relativists find themselves in conflict, there is, on their own showing, no neutral basis for comparison or assessment or mediation. Each is locked into their own way of thinking, and *ex hypothesi* can be given no neutrally based reason for abandoning that outlook or even questioning it. It is the absolutist who is committed to the view that any position can be assessed and criticized, and who therefore will find it easier to admit at least in principle that his own moral beliefs could be mistaken, and that the challenge presented by someone who equally sincerely holds incompatible moral beliefs is just the kind of stimulus that should invite both parties to re-examine their existing beliefs. That is just the atmosphere in which tolerance might better flourish.

Suppose, however, that someone were to claim that the enormous differences between cultures is itself a good argument to show that there can be no comparison between them. I think this approach offers a much better prospect of providing an argument for relativism. Even though in the end this argument, too, must ultimately fail, it needs to be very carefully considered. I wish to propose an analogy, and to develop two arguments in support of ethical relativism, each based on an analogy between ethics and sports. I hope that in developing these arguments as persuasively as I can, it will become clear exactly what the absolutist has to prove in order to refute them.

The first point the relativist might make has to do with the ambiguity of terms. The term "goal" refers to something different in association with football and in rugby: the ball has to go to a different place, and the number of points given when scoring a goal is different. The same is true for terms like "tackle" and "pass." The fact that the same words are used in the two sports could be very misleading for someone who tried to transfer unthinkingly from playing one kind of football to the other. Well, here is a moral parallel. About twenty years ago in London there was a celebrated controversy concerning a young girl of twelve in a local school. She shared with her classmates her experiences of home. It rapidly became evident that her home experiences were far from typical, in that she had recently come to Britain from another country, together with her husband. The British authorities were most unhappy about a man living with a girl under the age of sixteen; and when the husband protested that she was his wife, the authorities argued on the contrary that she could not be his wife, since she was only twelve years old, and a wife in Britain must be at least sixteen. Now a naive approach to this situation would be to ask "Was she his wife or wasn't she?" The reason why this approach is naive is that there is no one concept of "wife" shared between the two cultures in terms of which the question can be answered. Or, to put the same point in another way, it might be argued that there simply is no behaviour which could be the British equivalent of that man's relationship to that girl in their own culture. A British man who lived with a twelve-year-old girl in what he took to be a permanent relationship would still not be doing what the husband in my example would have been doing in his own culture. The actions are simply not comparable. The non-comparability of the actions explains the ambiguity of the term "wife." Here, then, is an argument for the crucial feature of relativism.

The analogy with sport can provide a second argument, this time a more general one. There will be some uncertainty, indeed disagreement, about precisely what is and what is not to count as a sport. There are clear cases, such as soccer, or athletics, or swimming. But how about mountaineering, or darts, or weightlifting, or ballroom dancing? At least sometimes, those who participate in one sport will not even be willing to consider another activity as a sport at all. I am told that in Spanish newspapers, accounts of bull-fights appear on the Arts Page; not on the Sports Page. There is a further and most important point. Each sport defines for itself what is worth doing, and what is to count as success. The virtues — notice that use of the term — of a good soccer team are quite different from those of a mountaineer or a javelin-thrower, and what it is for each of them to succeed is quite different again. A swimmer might have no desire whatsoever to be a good mountaineer, and a mountaineer might see no value at all in darts or bowls. Each sport inculcates its own values and methods and standards of success. There simply is no *sport-neutral* way of defining doing well, or the virtues proper to sports persons.

In a very similar way, the argument will run, different moralities define their own values internally. They set up ideals of what is and is not worth achieving, and what methods are permissible in trying to achieve what is given as worth while. So, the relativist will say, it will be difficult if not impossible for someone who has internalized one moral code to comprehend the values set out in another. Indeed, in extreme cases, it might be difficult for someone to recognize in another's conduct anything which would count as a morality at all. There was an article in the *New York Times Magazine* in 1997 (Oct. 12) about a young woman who was an *abd* in Mauritania. I use the term *abd* without translating it, since there is no translation in English which would correspond to the way the woman saw herself. In the article, the term was rendered as "slave." The young woman would say simply "God created me an *abd* just as he created a camel to be a camel." She had no concept of being *wrongly* treated, still less of being as we would say "enslaved"; she had no concept of freedom with which her position could be contrasted. When asked whether she had been raped, she had the greatest difficulty in understanding the question. "Of course they would come in the night when they needed to breed. Is that what you mean by 'rape'?" In her moral code, notions like slavery and rape and liberty simply made no sense, and she did not see herself as mistreated. These moral concepts of mine simply will not translate into her language. Or so it might be argued.

Just as it makes no sense to ask whether table-tennis is better than mountaineering, or marathon running is better than hang-gliding, or which sport embodies the true sporting values, so the moral relativist will want to argue that it makes no sense to ask which of several non-comparable codes of behaviour is the best, or which one recognizes the true moral values. The relativist maintains this position even in the case of moralities which resemble one another quite closely, just as it is in the case of sports such as rugby and soccer. So in ethics, it is clearly the case that many moral codes resemble one another to a high degree, while others are very different. But it still makes no sense to ask which of them is the best, because there is no morally neutral standard of what counts as best.

The version of relativism which stresses non-comparability has a lot to be said in its favour. It explains the particular combination of shocked disapproval and lack of comprehension which so often characterizes en-counters between members of different moral cultures. It explains, too, the difficulty which they so often have in finding any common ground on which they might stand in order to try to resolve their differences. It further explains why one natural response to confrontations of this kind is simply to deny that the other person has that kind of understanding — an *insider's* understanding — which is required to pass any judgments at all. Finally — and this is a consideration which seems to some philosophers to be a decisive advantage — the relativist picture is a very simple one. By that I mean that it makes no appeal to a special realm of moral facts over and above the perfectly ordinary facts concerning social conventions and long established language, habit and custom. It needs no further appeal to some obscure moral reality which makes some behaviour right or wrong, or some character trait to be a virtue rather than a vice. Every society needs some rules and conventions, but there is no particular set which every society needs, which might then be regarded as somehow the correct set, the true moral principles. So the absolutist can easily be pushed into the difficult position of explaining on what non-conventional basis morality is supposed to rest. As the history of philosophy amply shows, this is far from an easy question to answer convincingly. Such, then, is the argument which I will have to defeat in order to establish the non-relativist part of my thesis.

Let me return to the supposed parallel between moral codes and sports. One of the reasons why it is difficult to say what counts as a sport still less to rank sports in order of merit, is because there is no one aim which all sports have in common. Not all aim at fostering team spirit, or courage, or endurance, or self-discipline, or health. About all that they have in common is that in each of them it is possible to speak of being good or bad at it, or having developed the necessary skills. And that is such a general feature as to be quite unhelpful.

Well, is that a good parallel to the way in which we think of moral codes? The alleged parallel suggests that there is no uncontroversial and universal answer to questions such as "What is morality for?" or "With what is morality concerned?" But if there are acceptable answers to these questions, then at least the alleged parallel with a sport will break down. Moreover, it might be that the answers to these questions could provide us with a standard against which any particular moral code could be judged.

Answers are indeed forthcoming. One commonly proposed answer is that morality exists to promote social stability. A second answer is more ambitious. More than two millennia ago Aristotle argued that the point of what we call ethics (and he would have called ethics plus politics) is to enable us to live fulfilled lives, given that we are social and rational animals. In the last hundred years, several philosophers have returned to this Aristotelian view (though sometimes in a more individualistic mode than Aristotle himself would have approved), and argued that ethics without some concept of human fulfillment would be literally inconceivable. Morality has to have an intelligible *point*. It embodies our concept of fulfillment for ourselves as individuals living in a community.

Now I do not see how one can *prove* that the point of a set of moral beliefs is to articulate what it is to live a fulfilled life as a member of a community. But though I see no prospect of proving that it must be so, I do not think that this contention is seriously open to dispute. There must be some basic truths which it does not make genuine sense to question, and for which it makes no sense to ask for yet further support. But if it is not in dispute that the point of *any* morality has to do with the fulfillment of human beings as social and thinking animals, then at least it cannot be the case that moralities are *radically* incomparable. To that extent, a radical relativism turns out to be false, since the core of the relativist position is precisely non-comparability. Indeed it would be very surprising if different moral codes were strictly incomparable, for the problem at any rate as it has historically presented itself has always focused on the differences between moralities. There has not been any difficulty in recognizing alien belief systems *as moralities.* Anthropologists have surely succeeded in translating and therefore understanding what are clearly enough the moral codes of other societies. Indeed, the relativist himself has very often — inconsistently — attempted to use the differences between moral codes as evidence for relativism. I would argue that the fact that we can recognize different moralities not merely is not good evidence for relativism, but rather that it provides the basis for a refutation of relativism. If the moral codes of others can be translated and understood, however difficult and nuanced that task might be, and if they can be identified as moral codes in the first place, then radically incomparable they cannot be.

Absolutism and Human Nature

Of course, that answer in itself is not sufficient to provide a complete refutation of the relativist. It is still open to him to argue that even if all moral codes are comparable in that they all involve some notion of a fulfilled life, different moral codes are incomparably different in all the important ways because they embody *incomparably different conceptions* of fulfillment: and, crucially, because there is no way in which different conceptions of fulfillment can be neutrally assessed for correctness. So the absolutist needs a stronger argument to show that human fulfillment is not utterly beyond neutral assessment.

Aristotle's contention is that any notion of human fulfillment will in the end depend on an analysis of the internal goal directedness of human nature. Humans are like any other organisms in that they are characterized by a set of powers which are capable of functioning in a harmonized way which exhibits purposeful organization. This teleological view of the organic world was long rejected as fanciful and anthropomorphic; but at least to a considerable extent it has recently come back into fashion. Evolution, for instance, can in part be explained by the tendency of organisms to behave in such a way as to maximize the prospects of their genes being reproduced. On Aristotle's account, organisms flourish when their genetically determined organized powers function properly. In the case of humans, he believed that it is clear what these powers are: they can be classified in terms of physical health, reproduction, emotional health, and the existence of a system of trained desires and learnt needs which are both consistent with health and with the requirements of living in an organized society. In particular, Aristotle believed that the characteristic of human fulfillment was that it consisted of a life lived under the direction of a reflective and coherent understanding of what one was doing and why. The notion of a fulfilled life can therefore be spelt out in terms of a set of needs failure to satisfy which leads to damage — physical, emotional, or mental damage — plus a set of capacities which enables us to satisfy our needs in a rationally coherent and intelligible way.

That programme, so put, will doubtless strike different people in different ways. I shall address such differences in a few moments. At this point, however, I would like to stress that any intelligible version of ethics must have at its core some account of human fulfillment. Further, no account of human fulfillment can ignore the natural characteristics of human nature, and the ways in which the functioning of human individuals can be affected by various features in our several environments. In principle, the better we understand human physiology, psychology, and the patterns of social interaction, and the better we understand the ways in which we interact with our environment for better and for worse, the better placed we will be to provide fulfilled lives for one another.

In principle, then, it is possible to find a neutral basis for at least some assessments of different moral principles and codes. The question arises how far such assessments might be expected to take us. If, for the sake of argument, you grant the basically Aristotelian framework which I would endorse, then it will at once follow that the following values will be morally significant, since they form central constituents of human fulfillment: physical, emotional and mental health; moral and intellectual education without indoctrination or brainwashing; being permitted and indeed encouraged to make a recognizable contribution to the kind of society in which these values are consistently fostered. And if I had to pick just one, I would pick moral and intellectual education without indoctrination, since it is fundamental to all the others. In principle, this set of goals provides a basis for an assessment of any moral code. So, for example, the most fundamental criticism one would be fully entitled to make of an alien morality is that it attached little or no importance to the availability and standard of education which it sought to provide for as many people as possible. The society in which a young woman can grow up without having learnt even the notions of freedom, slavery, or rape, can justifiably be criticized as radically immoral, and cannot defeat that charge by saying that an outsider cannot possibly understand their values.

There are, however, several qualifications which need to be made. The first is that to say that these features of a human life are valuable is not quite to say that they are all absolutely indispensable for the living of a fulfilled life. There are exceptional cases. I have in mind, for instance, Christy Brown the award-winning Irish writer who is paralyzed in all four limbs and has to compose by using his head to move a stick onto a computer keyboard one letter at a time. It seems possible that the very need to overcome a physical disability can bring out very special qualities of personality and artistic imagination. Still, it would be a mistake to conclude from this that physical health is not important, or that it will in general be true that ill-health will prove a positive stimulus to personal development. Usually it will do nothing of the kind. What the example shows, I think, is that it is easy to over-generalize in ethics.

The second qualification is this: even if all the elements in a fulfilled life which I mentioned above are recognized as valuable and worth fostering, nothing follows about their relative importance, or the desirability of any particular "mix" for the achievement of a fulfilled life. At least on some interpretations, Aristotle attaches enormous importance to a person's intellectual development, and to the more theoretical side even of that. Others might think it just as important, or perhaps more important, to stress other activities such as family or community life, rather than intellectual speculation. The general point is that it is easy to think of a variety of ways of life, characterized by the widely differing emphasis placed on a commonly accepted set of values. So the recognition of those values does not of itself settle questions about their relative importance.

The third qualification is that it will all too often not be possible to promote all these values as fully across the whole of society, still less across the whole world, to the extent that one would wish, even in those cases in which we know how to do so. Shortage of resources, or other factors, might force us to choose between, for instance, promoting health or promoting education; or, again, between giving a more basic level of education to everyone, or providing higher education for some at the expense even of basic education for others. There are acute problems of distribution which are not solved simply by recognition of values which it is desirable to promote as widely as possible.

Nevertheless, and even with these qualifications, I suggest that an examination of the relationship between the nature of human beings and the ways in which that nature interacts with our various environments suggests that there are severe constraints on the ways in which it is possible for us to lead fulfilled lives, on any reasonable account of fulfillment. So, if it is true that the very notion of a morality must be based on some notion of a humanly fulfilled life, then there are constraints on any code which is recognizable as a morality. It is therefore perfectly possible to criticize some moral code for simply failing to take account of one or other of these values, either failing to promote it at all, or failing to promote it at all widely. It follows that it is also possible to criticize a moral code for failing to foster those traits of character which stabilize the recognition of those values in society. I have in mind such virtues as friendship, generosity, truthfulness, intellectual honesty, and justice.

So the general relativist position that no outsider can even in principle formulate any criticism of the moral code of another society is, I believe, demonstrably false. There is a common, though not morally neutral, basis for assessing all codes which claim to be moral codes. This basis consists in facts about human nature and the interaction between human nature and the environments in which humans live. These facts do not depend upon human convention, nor on what we might or might not happen to believe about ourselves or our environment.

To that extent, and in that sense, I wish to defend moral absolutism. Confusingly, the term "absolutism" is sometimes used to refer to the view that moral principles are true without any exceptions, or are true in all circumstances. I have no wish to defend moral absolutism in this latter sense.

Moral Absolutism and Moral Pluralism

I take moral pluralism to be the view that there might be more than one correct moral code. In this final section of my paper, I shall try to defend a pluralist view of ethics. There are several points at which morality might become pluralist. Time does not permit me to discuss all of them. I shall therefore make only a couple of brief remarks about the first two.

Each of the first two depends in one way or another upon our ignorance. In the first case, ignorance of admittedly relevant non-moral facts — about human physiology, or psychology, or about economics, or about genetics, and so on. In a condition of ignorance, it might easily be the case that well-supported arguments can be made for more than one course of action, or policy, or moral principle, and that we simply are not in a position to decide between them.

It follows that incompatible moral views can be equally rationally defended. That is one form of pluralism. The same general remarks will apply to cases where the ignorance is philosophical rather than straightfor-wardly factual — as for instance concerning the various possible criteria for defining death.

These two types of pluralism might be called pluralism of the equally defensible. I would like to spend a little more time on arguments for a more radical form of pluralism, which I might term pluralism of the equally correct. Is there any reason to suppose that a moral absolutist has to hold that there is only *one* moral code which could offer individuals or society the prospect of fostering ideally fulfilled lives? Or is it the case that there might be more than one morality, that they might be in some ways incompatible, and yet that they might all be equally true?

The very suggestion might seem obviously absurd. For consider, this debate is being conducted on the assumption that moral statements have truth-values; it surely follows that incompatible moral statements must have opposite truth-values: the suggestion that statements with opposite truth-values can all be true is simply absurd and can be dismissed at once. But I think there are reasons to suppose that this difficulty is not fatal. Remember that the point of any morality is to identify what it is to live a fulfilled life. In order to do this, it will prescribe certain traits of character as desirable, certain patterns of emotional response as balanced and helpful, certain values as worth promoting, and so on. Living a fulfilled life is a complex activity — or rather it consists in a complex set of activities linked together into an intentional whole which makes coherent sense. So the question is this: is there just one way of living which is truly fulfilling for human beings? More precisely, in any given environment is there for each person only one life which could be truly fulfilling for that person? It seems to me that there is every reason to suppose that the answer to this question is "No." Several considerations might be thought to point in this direction. People have changed their way of living in mid-life and have found their later way of living just as fulfilling as their earlier one. Again, most of us could imagine our lives as having gone differently, without necessarily having to suppose that they would thereby have been either more or less fulfilling than the life we in fact have. And, more radically, we might have met people who actually live fulfilled lives in very different types of society — in remote farming communities, in large urban settings, in tribal villages, and so on. Evidence of this kind, vague though it is, seems to me at least to suggest that humans are very flexible and adaptable; they can find very different ways of living genuinely fulfilling. Indeed, such adaptability is one of the most striking characteristics of human beings.

In particular, there are many ways in which we can successfully decide the emphasis to be given to the various potentially conflicting needs which we experience. Most obviously, there are various possible ways of balancing the competing claims of imagination and the emotions, the demands of practical affairs, and the claims of the intellect. A person can live a fulfilled life as, let us say, a pianist, or an actor, or as a carpenter or in business or politics, or in research into the foundations of mathematics. It is possible to be fulfilled by marrying and rearing a family, or by remaining single and having a wide circle of friends. And so on. I incline to think not merely that different people will find fulfillment in very different kinds of life: indeed, there is every reason to suppose that the same person might be equally fulfilled in more than one kind of life.

Secondly, different cultures might adopt different views about the most just way of resolving difficulties arising from the competing claims of individuals against one another, and between claims to individual liberties and the good of society as a whole. It has often been pointed out that nowhere in Aristotle's writings on ethics and politics is there any obvious concern for the individual liberties or the human rights so dear to the contemporary Westerner. Some societies value cohesion, stability and cooperation more than individual initiative, innovation and independence. There have been attempts to base theories of justice on rights, on needs, and on deserts. There are more liberal Rawlsian theories, and more conservative theories in the manner of Nozick. It is a plain fact, however, that despite the enormous attention which has been paid to the question in the last thirty years, not merely is there no one acceptable theory of justice, but there seems to be no agreed mechanism even for reaching an agreed view of justice. While this indeed does not prove that there is no one correct theory of justice waiting to be found, it does perhaps suggest that there might well be more than one rationally defensible view, and perhaps even that there are several patterns of justice each of which is morally acceptable. A fulfilled society, so to speak, might be just as pluralist a notion as a fulfilled individual life.

Finally, and even more briefly, a consequence of these differences is likely to be that the qualities of character and intellect — the virtues, in short, which are recognized and fostered in a society — will often be notably different from those valued in another society. Examples might be the ideals of maleness exemplified in the heroes of the Homeric epics, or in the *machismo* of some Latin countries in our own day; the ancient Roman concept of *pietas;* the notions of honour, both male and female, found in Europe in the seventeenth and eighteenth centuries, contemporary virtues such as coolness; Christian humility. These various virtues fit into different conceptions of the fulfilled life and of the society in which such a life can flourish. Not all of them are equally defensible, I am sure. Moreover, not all of them are readily transferable from one social context into another. For it is characteristic of different conceptions of fulfillment that the various elements which are thought to be constitutive of the fulfilled life are not wholly independent of one another: they gain their importance and meaning as much from their inter-relationships as from their intrinsic nature. It is often misleading to evaluate any one element in isolation; a fulfilled life involves a system of checks and balances, and a set of interacting meanings and aims.

That concludes my case for pluralism. By way of conclusion to this essay, I would like to emphasize that the pluralism for which I have argued is a pluralism within an absolutist framework. The one human nature which we all share, and whose genetic characteristics serve to distinguish us from other animals, is a highly flexible and adaptable nature. Perhaps the physical basis for this is the much larger brain size which characterizes humans. This natural fact might explain why there are for humans many ways of living a fulfilled life, many more than there are for other organisms. But there are also many ways of living which could not on any account be considered as fulfilling; human beings are not infinitely flexible nor indefinitely malleable. Again, though there may be several satisfactory views of justice, there are also many ways of treating individuals, and many ways of structuring society, which are demonstrably unjust, as I hope was illustrated by the tragic example of the Mauritanian girl whom I mentioned earlier. Flexible as we humans are, it is a shared nature which we all have, and it is that shared nature which defines the parameters within which any successful system of ethics must operate. Moreover, it is those parameters which provide the basis on which any system can be evaluated, whether by insiders or by outsiders. That there is such a basis follows from the refutation of relativism. But that more than one morality can be constructed which will truly contribute to human fulfillment is a consequence of the richness of the nature which we all share.

Cultural and Ecological Consequences of Globalizing Computers

C. A. Bowers

The rate and scale of change associated with computers has overwhelmed the ability of most people to ask whether the forms of knowledge and community relationships being undermined by this technology are essential to a culturally diverse and ecologically sustainable future. This question is profoundly different from present concerns about security issues that computers create for corporations and governments, and the privacy issues that citizens now face. New fire walls can be designed to protect the electronic infrastructures that corporations and governments now depend upon, and governments can enact legislation that protects citizens from having information about their private lives sold in the marketplace of cyberspace. These are largely issues that can be settled through further technological development. The cultural changes resulting from computer mediated thought and communication are of a different order: one that does not lend itself to finding new technological solutions.

The suggestion that the cultural patterns being displaced by computers may, over the long term, be more important than the vast economic opportunities associated with computers appears especially difficult to reconcile with the widely held Western myth that equates change with a linear form of progress. This myth, which was part of the ideology that gave conceptual direction and moral legitimacy to the Industrial Revolution, has been strengthened by the merging of Western Enlightenment assumptions with the scientific evidence of evolution that is now being fashioned into a powerful meta-narrative. The assumptions of Enlightenment thinkers have served as the seedbed of what Edward Shils has referred to as the "anti-tradition traditions of thinking that still flourish in Western universities." (Shils, 1981:287) The meta-narrative of evolution combines solid scientific evidence with the hubris of well-known scientists who neither understand the Janus nature of science nor the deep symbolic foundations of their own culture. As we can see in such books as Richard Dawkins' *The*

Selfish Gene (1976), Francis Crick's *The Astonishing Hypothesis: The Scientific Search for the Soul* (1994), Carl Sagan's *The Demon-haunted World: Science as a Candle in the Dark* (1997), and E. O. Wilson's *Consilience: The Unity of Knowledge* (1998), scientists who think within the framework of the evolution meta-narrative have little interest in considering the forms of knowledge and community that are being displaced by modern science and technology.

If we examine the cultural mediating characteristics of computers by using an interpretative framework that is not based on Enlightenment assumptions, we can more easily recognize how computers continue the process of colonization that was a hallmark of the Industrial Revolution. That is, we can recognize computers as representing the latest stage in the development and expansion of the Industrial Revolution that began with the factory system in early nineteenth-century England. Computers represent the digital phase of this historical process, and not a radical break from the past that is suggested in such phrases as the "Information Age."

Computers have led to profound changes in the workplace, and between manufacturers and markets, even while they continue to perpetuate other key characteristics of the Industrial Revolution. The earlier drive to control the source of natural resources upon which the industrial process depended has not been substantially changed. In overcoming the obstacles of time, space, and national boundaries that were part of the colonial era, the Internet now makes it possible for corporations to achieve even greater efficiencies in the integration of raw materials, low-wage manufacturing sites, and mass markets. The period of Western colonization is supposedly behind us; but the Western model of development remains the core feature of what is now being called "globalization."

This model of development has as its aim the creation of a monoculture of thought patterns, values, and forms of dependency. A key feature of this monoculture is the relentless energy that is directed toward commodifying all aspects of individual and community life.

Computer-based globalization is accelerating the transformation of the market, which in traditional cultures was often limited to a particular day and physical location within the community. Writing from a Third World perspective, Gerald Berthoud notes that the ideology of the industrial model of development requires the acceptance that "we are all subject to the compelling idea that everything that can be made must be made, and then sold. Our universe (must appear) unshakably structured by the omnipotence of techno-scientific truth and the laws of the market." (Berthoud, 1992:71)

Berthoud goes on to note that the industrial ideology which promotes unlimited consumerism requires fundamental changes in the moral foundations of non-Western culture:

> What must be universalized through (the Western model of) development is a cultural complex centered around [sic] the notion that human life, if it is to be fully lived, cannot be constrained by limits of any kind. To produce such a result in traditional societies, for whom the supposedly primordial principle of boundless expansion in the technological and economic domains is generally alien, presupposes overcoming symbolic and moral "obstacles," that is ridding these societies of various inhibiting ideas and practices such as myths, ceremonies, rituals, mutual aid, networks of solidarity, and the like. (Berthoud, 1992:72)

While these forms of knowledge represent sources of resistance to the Western model of economic development and hyper-consumerism, they are viewed by scientists such as Dawkins, Crick, Sagan, and Wilson as pre-scientific and thus as representative of earlier stages in the process of cultural evolution.

Before examining how the forms of knowledge privileged by the mediating characteristics of computers contribute to undermining the "symbolic and moral obstacles" to accepting consumerism as the most progressive way of meeting daily life needs, it is necessary to highlight the form of individualism required by a technology-consumer-dependent culture. In *Rebels Against the Future: The Luddites and Their War on the Industrial Revolution* (1995), Kirkpatrick Sale summarizes how traditional interdependencies within communities, which varied from culture to culture, had to be undermined in order to create the kind of individual who would be easily manipulated as a consumer:

> All that "community" implies — self-sufficiency, mutual aid, morality in the market place, stubborn tradition, regulation by custom, organic knowledge instead of mechanistic science — had to be steadily and systematically disrupted and displaced. All of the practices that kept the individual from becoming a consumer had to be done away with so that the cogs and wheels of an unfettered machine called "the economy" could operate without interference, influenced merely by invisible hands and inevitable balances. (Sale, 1995:38)

It is important to note that this autonomous form of individualism has been the goal both of liberal and conservative approaches to education in the West. That is, they both identify rational decision-making, including moral judgments, as the defining capacity of the autonomous individual. In short, their educational ideal of the empowered individual is un-encumbered by communal traditions of moral reciprocity and inter-generational knowledge. It is, in fact, identical to the type of individual that Sale describes as being essential to the success of the Industrial Revolution.

Especially noteworthy is how leading proponents justify computers on the grounds that they foster this rootless form of individualism. They even go a step further by claiming that cyberspace frees the individual from the accountability that is part of face-to-face communities, which they view as an advancement in human development. For example, Sherry Turkle, a professor of sociology at MIT and the author of *Life on the Screen: Identity in the Age of the Internet* (1995), writes that:

> I have argued that Internet experiences help us to develop models of psychological well-being that are in a meaningful sense postmodern: They admit of multiplicity and flexibility. They acknowledge the constructed nature of reality, self, and other. The Internet is not alone in encouraging such models. There are many places within our culture that do so. What they have in common is that they all suggest the value of approaching one's "story" in several ways and with fluid access to one's different aspects. We are encouraged to think of ourselves as fluid, emergent, decentralized, multiplicitous, flexible, and ever in process. (Turkle, 1995:263–64)

Turkle is not alone in recognizing that computers reinforce the ex-perience of being free from the interdependent relationships of community.

Harold Rheingold, the author of *Virtual Reality* (1991) and a co-founder of one of the first electronic communities in the San Francisco Bay Area called the WELL, explains the differences between cyberspace and face-to-face communities in the following way:

> On top of the technology-imposed constraints, we who populate cyberspace deliberately experiment with fracturing traditional notions of identity by living multiple simultaneous personae in different virtual neighborhoods. We reduce and encode our identities as words on a screen, decode and unpack the identities of others. The way we use these words, in stories (true and false) we tell about ourselves (or about the identities we want people to believe us to be), is what determines our identities in cyberspace. (Rheingold, 1991:61)

The cultural schemata reproduced in this account of his personal experience in cyberspace is one that is largely taken for granted by mem-bers of the dominant, high-status culture in the West.

What Turkle and Rheingold fail to recognize is that the replacement of the traditional face-to-face formation of identity with the context-free, highly subjective and experimental identity is only imaginable in cultures where the relentless pursuit of change and experimentation are interpreted as expressions of progress. Furthermore, viewing individuals as authoring their own "reality" within a context that does not involve some form of social accountability, not to mention accountability to the biotic community that sustains life "off-line," is comprehensible only in a culture that mistakenly represents the individual as not being dependent upon the symbolic and natural ecologies we are all embedded in. Rheingold's acceptance of a machine mediated relationship also requires a taken-for-granted cultural schemata that has lost touch with the importance of communal memory that, in many cultures, carries forward the wisdom of fundamental relationships gleaned from centuries of experience of the continuities and changes in the environment. That cultures in the real world, such as the indigenous cultures in North and South America, as well as cultures in China, India, Southeast Asia, and Africa, are experiencing the consequences of degraded natural systems also needs to be recognized in any discussion of the freedoms made possible in cyberspace.

The contrast between Rheingold's celebration of the possibilities of cyberspace and the insights that John Berger, the British art critic, gained from living with a group of peasants in rural France is particularly relevant here. Berger noted that the conservatism of the peasant lifestyle was rooted in a deep awareness that scarcity, given the unpredictableness of environmental conditions, is an ever present possibility. Reflecting upon the view of progress taken-for-granted in modern ideologies, as well as by people living in modern, urban settings, Berger concluded that the experimentally based lifestyle is predicated on the false cultural premise that progress is not dependent upon the contingencies of natural systems. (Berger, 1979:204) Rheingold's account of creating community in cyberspace reflects the affluent, progressive, and experimental mind-set that is based on this cultural assumption.

Before considering the forms of knowledge and relationships reinforced by the cultural mediating characteristics of computers, it is first necessary to consider more closely how the meta-narrative of evolution is now being linked to computers in a way that gives the appearance of scientific legitimacy to the "survival of the fittest" ideology that underlies the current economic and technological process of globalization. Like the earlier phases of the Industrial Revolution, the creation of global markets based on the new electronic infrastructure of communication also requires the globalization of Western assumptions about the nature of the individual, the material source of happiness, and the need to view intergenerational knowledge and responsibility as outmoded. By interpreting the development and spread of computers as part of the evolutionary process of natural selection, which computer ideologues interpret wrongly as a linear form of progress, the possibility is further undermined that the forms of knowledge and community relationships that cannot be communicated through a computer will be taken seriously. As the following quotations make clear, the cultural patterns that cannot be digitalized and thus commodified have not met the test of Darwinian fitness, and thus must be left behind.

These quotations should also be viewed as further examples of scientists who are extrapolating from their fields of expertise the direction that cultural change should take. In not understanding the complexity of the cultural traditions their ideology consigns to the category of recent extinctions, they are providing conceptual and moral legitimacy to the formation of a global monoculture that will, over the short term, increase the market for the products of transnational corporations. Ironically, the creation of a monoculture ignores a fundamental truth that is at the heart of the evolutionary process — one that also applies to cultures: namely, that ecosystems thrive on diversity. A diversity of cultural ways of knowing that encode the intergenerational experience of the limits and possibilities of a bioregion is, in effect, the best guarantee against undermining the diversity of natural systems — especially when the alternative is a monoculture based on an industrial model that encourages hyperconsumerism.

The use of an evolutionary framework to explain how computers fit into Nature's process of design is now being adopted by a number of scientists. One of the most troubling explanations of how computers represent the evolutionary transition to a "post-biological world" of "thinking machines" can be found in Hans Moravec's book, *Mind Children: The Future of Robot and Human Intelligence* (1988). After providing an overview of the major transitions in the evolution of life, Moravec goes on to say:

> Our culture still depends utterly on biological human beings, but with each passing year our machines, a major product of the culture, assume a greater role in its maintenance and continued growth.

> Sooner or later our machines will become knowledgeable enough to handle their own maintenance, reproduction, and self-improvement without help. When this happens, the new genetic takeover will be complete. Our culture will then be able to evolve independently of human biology and its limitations, passing instead directly from generation to generation of ever more capable intelligent machinery. (Moravec, 1988:4)

Especially noteworthy is his reference to "our culture," as though there is only one "culture" and that as a scientist and Nature's chief design agent he has the right to participate in efforts to develop technologies that will replace humans in the evolutionary process with thinking machines.

The title of Gregory Stock's book, *Metaman: The Merging of Humans and Machines into a Global Superorganism* (1993), is equally disturbing. Like Moravec, he also uses an evolutionary framework to explain the extinction of the world's cultures. As he puts it, "Today, such diversity is mostly a thing of the past." (p. 99) What is emerging is a human-machine hybrid he calls "Metaman." As the nature of human beings begins to change, he continues, so too will concepts of what it means to be human. One day humans will be composite beings: "part biological, part mechanical, part electronic." (p. 152) The emergence of Metaman, which is the superorganism that Stock sees emerging on a global basis, is explained in the following way:

> Metaman, like a developing organism, manifests change within itself rather than its progeny, but Metaman changes by unprogrammed adaptation that is decidedly evolutionary in character. Metaman's ability to evolve so rapidly is the result of three key enhancements of Darwinian mechanisms. First, Metaman has internalized natural selection. External competition among separate organism has given way to internal competition among component elements of the superorganism. Second, conscious design has supplanted random variation. Because products are invented, corporate organizations planned, and machines designed, there is no need to wait for random "happy accidents." Third, competition among real, material entities has been joined by competition among abstract representations (concepts, ideas, and plans). (Stock, 1993:227–28)

The technology that is to serve as the brain and central nervous system of this global superorganism is the computer.

Though not a scientist himself, Kevin Kelly's book *Out of Control: The Rise of Neo-biological Civilization* (1994) reiterates the role that Nature plays in the development and spread of computer-based technologies. As the founder of *Wired* magazine, which is one of the more influential publications within the sub-culture of the computer industry, Kelly's ideas of how computers fit into the larger scheme of things should be considered as widely shared. Indeed, the concluding statement in his book provides the ultimate legitimacy for their work. For computer devotees who might wonder about the political and moral issues that members of other cultures might raise about the transforming nature of computers, Kelly provides the following assurance: "we should not be surprised that life, having subjugated the bulk of inert matter on Earth, would go on to subjugate technology (including the computer), and bring it also under its reign of constant evolution, perpetual novelty, and an agenda out of our control." (Kelly, 1994:472)

"Evolution," like the earlier god-words of "progress" and "modernization," thus makes questioning and resistance futile — if not reactionary.

Even more remarkable and disturbing is Raymond Kurzweil's most recent book, *The Age of Spiritual Machines: When Computers Exceed Human Intelligence* (1999). On downloading the human mind into a computer, he writes that "when we scan someone's brain and reinstate their personal mind file in a suitable computing medium, the newly emergent "person" will appear to observers to have very much the same personality, history, memory as the personal originally scanned. (Kurzweil, 1999:125) Another prediction is that computational technology will make human mortality a thing of the past, as the technology will have the capacity to continually redesign itself. Kurzweil also claims:

> With the next stage of evolution creating a new generation of humans that will be trillions of times more capable and complex than humans today, our ability for spiritual experience and insight is likely to gain in power and depth. Twenty-first century machines — based on the design of human thinking, will do as their human progenitors have done "going to real and virtual houses of worship, meditating, praying, and transcending" to connect with their spiritual dimensions. (Kurzweil, 1999:152–53)

As the quotations demonstrate, the messianic spirit that once drove the expansion of Christianity has now become secularized and taken over by scientists who do not understand that while evolution can explain the interplay of continuities and chance in the development of organisms, it cannot provide answers to questions that are fundamentally political and moral in nature — questions made even more complex by differences in cultural ways of knowing.

Several key points need to be reiterated here. Representing the development and spread of computers as the next stage in the evolution of life is dependent upon three assumptions that need to be challenged. First, that only those cultures that transform themselves in the radical way required by computer mediated thought and communication meet the test of Darwinian fitness and thus deserve to survive. Second, that computers are, like other technologies, culturally neutral and that their global spread does not represent a continuation of Western colonization. Third, that the global spread of the mindset reinforced by computers does not need to take into account how a consumer, technologically dependent lifestyle will impact the viability of the Earth's ecosystems. In the rest of this essay, I will challenge all three assumptions by explaining how computers, by their very nature, reinforce culturally specific patterns of thinking and communicating — and in the process undermine cultures that have developed approaches to community that have a more ecologically sustainable footprint. In short, I will explain how computers reinforce the cultural patterns required by the Industrial Revolution, and thus increase the ecological risks facing future generations — even as computers enable us to perform technological marvels that were unimaginable a decade or so ago.

Just as the technological characteristics of the telephone determines that voice will be selected for amplification over distance, while eliminating the embodied aspects of meta-communication from the process of communication, computers have inherent characteristics that amplify certain cultural patterns of thinking and communicating, while simultaneously reducing and eliminating others. The cultural patterns that are amplified correspond to what Western universities have elevated as high-status knowledge, while the patterns that are reduced or eliminated are regarded as expressions of low-status knowledge — which are studied in universities for purposes of understanding primitive cultures and folk practices. (Bowers, 1997) It must be emphasized here that the following list of amplification and reduction characteristics are inherent in the nature of computer technology, and are not the result of misapplying the technology. It also needs to be emphasized that current efforts to incorporate emotional and olfactory aspects of experience into computer software (Picard, 1997) will never be able to duplicate the contextual nature of embodied experience in which different cultural patterns are reenacted — for the most part, cultural patterns that the people who write the software are not aware of.

The following is a list of amplification and reduction characteristics of computer technology:

(1) *Computers can only process explicit and de-contextualized thoughts, forms of expression, and cultural patterns.*

Cultural patterns that are taken for granted, including the contextual and accompanying complexity of meta-communication about the relationships between the patterns and physical environment, cannot be digitalized. Thus, they cannot be communicated through a computer. When the patterns are made explicit and digitalized, they are then taken out of the context of shared meanings and tacit understandings of traditional relationships and moral norms — which means they become abstract and fundamentally changed. The key issue here is that tacit cultural patterns and understandings, including the patterns of meta-communication, encode different cultural ways of knowing and historical experiences.

In *Hombres y Machos*, Alfredo Mirande gives the example of the word *pelado* that defies simple translation. While it literally means "plucked," "naked" or "stripped," and connotes a lowly person, a nobody, Mirande notes that it encodes the historical memory of the rape and devastation of the Spanish Conquistadors; it also denotes both positive and negative qualities — depending upon the context in which it is used. (Mirande, 1997:37–39) The context, perspective, layers of class and gendered memory, and intent behind the use of the word are eliminated by the mediating characteristics of the computer. The power of the computer is in transforming the deeply contextual and cultural into what can be abstractly represented on the screen. Just as the printed word played a powerful role in shaping the West's understanding of what should be regarded as high and low-status knowledge, the computer simply perpetuates this tradition of discrimination against oral traditions. Giving computers the ability to communicate in scripted voices will not fundamentally alter the fact that context and tacit cultural understandings cannot be programmed.

(2) *Computers amplify a way of thinking that assumes that data is the basis of thought and that language (words, grammatical patterns) is a neutral technology that allows ideas, information, and data to be communicated to others.*

To make this key point more directly, it is impossible for computers to be programmed in such a way that the history and culturally specific nature of the metaphorical language appearing on the screen can be made explicit. Nor can the computer be programmed to interact with the interpretation that the individual brings to the metaphorical language appearing on the screen. That is, computers reinforce the representational function of language. This view of language, which is essential to sustaining the West's high-status cultural myth of objective knowledge, involves the assumption that words stand for and thus represent real entities and have universal meanings. At the same time, computers put out of focus the metaphorical nature of language — that is, that language encodes the root metaphors and earlier processes of analogic thinking of a cultural group. That the elites of other cultures often communicate in ways that are easily understood by Western thinkers, which reinforces the myth of words having universal meanings, can be explained by the fact that they have been largely educated in Western universities and think within the epistemic patterns of the English language — which is further reinforced when communicated through a computer.

(3) *The conduit view of language, the privileging of print-based thought and communication, the decontextualized nature of the words and visual models appearing on the screen serve to reinforce the Western assumption that the individual is an autonomous social being.*

These mediating characteristics strengthen the Western cultural emphasis on subjective perspective, interpretation, and choice as being hallmarks of our autonomous individuality. The experience of self as integral to a dynamic web of reciprocal relationships, or as having an identity that is inclusive of the extended family (and even a cultural group), cannot be communicated through a computer. Regardless of whether it is the printed word appearing on the screen or interaction with a scripted voice that does not have a regional accent, the computer reinforces the Western view of the individual who has a distinct perspective, makes choices in terms of the options made available by the computer program — including the choice to turn off the computer, and reflect on the experience. The amplification of the experience of being an autonomous decision maker, in turn, further reinforces other Western cultural assumptions — including an anthropocentric relationship with the environment and that values are a matter of individual choice and responsibility.

(4) *Computer-mediated thought and communication reinforces the modern, individually-centred experience of temporality: that is, how the past, present, and future are experienced.*

Computers, like earlier print-based technology, reinforce the Western cultural experience of a spectator relationship to the past and future. What computers foster is the sense that it is the present moment in time that provides the vantage point for looking back or into the future, and deciding whether either one should be taken into account in terms of the immediate moment of decision making. To put this in another way, whether the past and future have any relevance is contingent on the emotive and rational judgment of the individual. This is radically different from the experience of temporality in other cultures where both the past and future are experienced as part of the living present. The traditional practice of some indigenous cultures in North America of framing decisions in terms of the well-being of the seventh unborn generation contrasts sharply with the experience of temporality reinforced by computers. Examples of cultures that experience the past as an integral part of the present are even more numerous. Current efforts to recover the ancient agricultural practices in the Andes is an example of indigenous people using the past as a source of empowerment. (Apffel-Marglin, 1998)

While modern individuals are engaged in computer-mediated activities, they are enacting simultaneously a wide range of traditions that are not recognized as traditions because of their taken-for-granted status. And because these traditions (spellings, use of paragraphs, layout of the keyboard, use of root metaphors, and so forth) have become integral to their natural attitude toward everyday life, they are present sources of empowerment. But the way computers reinforce how being-in-time is experienced puts out of focus the many ways in which traditions are re-enacted and given individualized interpretation. In effect, computers foster what can only be called an illusory sense of time which, in turn, contributes to diverting awareness from the many viable traditions that are being undermined by the different applications of computer technology. For example, the traditional norms governing the distinction between our private and public life have been disappearing with each "advance" in the use of computers. The way in which computers amplify the modern bias that traditions are restrictive and outmoded, while at the same time reinforcing an awareness of time that is subjectively determined, ensures that the value of traditions will not be recognized until after they have been lost. At that point, they cannot be recovered — which is not worrisome for the citizen of cyberspace. For members of cultural groups that still experience traditions and the future as sources of authority and responsibility in making decisions, using the computer can be a conflicted experience — especially if they still value the traditions that are the basis of their sense of community and self-identity.

(5) *The fact that computers must be purchased, and that there are other costs connected with their use and upgrades, means that they involve the commodification of the most basic activities and relationships: thought and communication.*

Even if computers were made freely available to everybody they still would be part of the industrial culture — and they would still operate as a cultural colonizing technology. The current rush to turn cyberspace into an electronic shopping mall and thus to further undermine the economic viability of the small and medium size businesses that constitute the center of towns and cities, indicates how computers make consumerism an even more ubiquitous aspect of people's lives. The traditional nature of shopping, when done in the town centre, provides for social interaction that knits the community together. Shopping on the Internet, while seemingly more convenient, further reduces the need to interact with other people — where a wide range of issues and events might become part of the conversation. It also eliminates the small producer and other workers who are necessary in the economic life of the community. The Internet, in effect, further strengthens the trend toward centralization of production and distribution of goods and services in ways that maximize the economy of scale for corporations. At the same time, the Internet reduces the accountability and community building relationships characteristic of small scale local producers. (Bowers, 2000)

As suggested earlier, the above list of amplification characteristics — print-based decontextualized thought — the autonomous individual who relies upon data as the source of ideas, an individually-centred view of time which makes traditions and the future contingent upon subjective mood and rational self-interest, a view of language that reinforces the assumption that intelligence is an individual attribute rather than the individualizing of a shared cultural episteme — needs to be examined in terms of the antecedents of the characteristics. What comes immediately to mind are the similarities between Kirkpatrick Sale's description of the type of individual required by the early phase of the Industrial Revolution and the form of individualism reinforced by computers. And just as there was then a conflict and eventual assimilation that had disastrous consequences for the environment, there continues to be a conflict between the digital phase of the Industrial Revolution and cultural groups who are attempting to resist the pressures of Western modernism. Indeed, the failed efforts of the Luddites are a metaphor for today's process of globalization.

Just as the list of computer mediating characteristics corresponds to what is required for a consumer-oriented culture, the list of what cannot be digitalized matches with many of the characteristics of cultural groups that have developed their own approaches to relative self-sufficient communities. The latter includes the face-to-face activities that represent the whole range of non-commodified activities and relationships that constitute the life of the community: forms of knowledge and relationships essential to learning the norms governing moral reciprocity; narratives of how the ecologies of family and community are anchored in the ecologies of place; modelling how to perform certain activities and the longer process of mentoring that combines the development of character with the development of individual talents; participating in the ceremonies that renew the community's symbolic and moral foundations; learning the patterns of meta-communication that strengthen relationships and facilitate communication; participating in the intergenerational life of the community in ways that discard outmoded and wrongly constituted traditions while renewing others — and creating new ones that take into account the well-being of future generations. The wide variation in how these participatory and embodied patterns of community are expressed by different cultural groups cannot be communicated through a computer. However, they can be digitalized in a documentary format. Others can learn from them and even view them as a source of entertainment. But the fact remains that while many people may view this documentation as a contribution to an educational process it is also part of the process of commodification that reinforces the cultural patterns associated with the autonomous individual who enters the experience as a spectator.

In identifying the patterns of face-to-face community life that cannot be communicated through a computer without becoming transformed into an abstract, decontextualized representation, I am not suggesting that all community patterns (mentoring, narrativizing, ceremonies, and so forth) are morally equal and environmentally viable. Recent experience in the Balkans and other parts of the world suggest that this is not the case. Nor am I suggesting that all forms of electronic communities can be dismissed because they reinforce a particular form of individualism and cultural way of knowing. Rather, the point is more fundamental — namely, that the very nature of computers leads to certain cultural patterns being reinforced over others. This should lead, in turn, to asking how the cultural patterns reinforced, as well as those marginalized or directly undermined, impact the environment, the quality of community life, and the diversity of the world's cultures.

A strong case can be made that a technology that fosters a global monoculture of autonomous individuals who are dependent upon consumerism, which in turn accelerates the destruction of the environment, will indeed influence the process of evolution — but in a way that undermines the long-term chances of human survival. Cultural diversity, local knowledge, traditions of moral reciprocity, intergenerational knowledge and skills that limit the need for consumerism are more likely to meet the test of Darwinian fitness.

References

Apffel-Marglin, Frederique, ed. (1998). *The Spirit of Regeneration: Andean Culture Confronting Western Notions of Development.* London: Zed Books.

Berger, John (1979). *Pig Earth.* New York: Pantheon Books.

Berthoud, Gerald (1992). "Market." Wolfgang Sachs, ed., *The Development Dictionary: A Guide to Knowledge as Power.* London: Zed Books.

Bowers, C. A. (1997). *The Culture of Denial: Why the Environmental Movement Needs a Strategy for Reforming Universities and Public Schools.* Albany, New York: State University of New York Press.

——— (2000). *Let Them Eat Data: Ecological and Educational Consequences of Globalizing Computer Culture.* Athens, Georgia: University of Georgia Press.

Crick, Francis (1994). *The Astonishing Hypothesis: The Scientific Search for the Soul.* New York: Charles Scribner's Sons.

Dawkins, Richard (1976). *The Selfish Gene.* New York: Oxford University Press.

Kelly, Kevin (1994). *Out of Control: The Rise of Neo-biological Civilization.* Reading, Massachusetts: Addison-Wesley.

Kurzweil, Raymond (1999). *The Age of Spiritual Machines: When Computers Exceed Human Intelligence.* New York: Viking Press.

Mirande, Alfredo (1997). *Hombres y Machos: Masculinity and Latino Culture.* Boulder, Colorado: Westview Press.

Moravec, Hans (1988). *Mind Children: The Future of Robot and Human Intelligence.* Cambridge, Massachusetts: Harvard University Press.

Picard, Rosalind W. (1997). *Affective Computing.* Cambridge, Massachusetts: MIT Press.

Rheingold, Harold (1991). *Virtual Reality.* New York: Summit Books.

——— (1993). "A Slice of Life in My Virtual Community." Linda M. Harasim, ed., *Global Networks: Computers and International Communication.* Cambridge, Massachusetts: MIT Press.

Sagan, Carl (1997). *The Demon Haunted World: Science as a Candle in the Dark.* London: Headline Book.

Sale, Kirpatrick (1995). *Rebels Against the Future: The Luddites and Their War on the Industrial Revolution.* Reading, Massachusetts: Addison-Wesley.

Shils, Edward (1981). *Tradition.* Chicago: University of Chicago Press.

Stock, Gregory (1993). *Metaman: The Merging of Humans and Machines into a Global Organism.* Toronto: Doubleday Canada.

Turkle, Sherry (1996). *Life on the Screen: Identity in the Age of the Internet.* New York: Simon and Schuster.

Wilson, Edward O. (1998). *Consilience: The Unity of Knowledge.* New York: Alfred A. Knopf.

Revitalization of Cultural Legacies in Northeast Asia

Shuichi Kato

One thousand years ago, the Lady Murasaki, a Japanese noblewoman, wrote a long story describing the romantic exploits of one Prince Genji, a hero. This work turned out to be the first modern novel, in that it described the psychology of a person against the background of daily life, and was not purely a fantastic or miraculous story. A thousand years ago she would not have thought of having it printed and circulated amongst the larger public since there was no printing system and there was no way that she could have ever imagined taking an airplane from Kyoto to Hong Kong to deliver a message at a university, since the only flying beings were Daoist immortals. How can I make any kind of prediction at the dawn of the third millennium? Therefore, I would like to reign in my subject, and talk about some possibilities for the next hundred years.

As my knowledge and the time available is limited, I will confine my subject, not to the world generally, but to the region where I have lived most of my life: northeast Asia. One thousand years ago, the major protagonists were China, Korea and Japan, just as they are now. I will begin with a brief sketch of the present situation in the region and will deal first with economics. The economic future seemed rosy in the twentieth century, since this region was abundant in natural and human resources, with high levels of education, higher than other places except perhaps for Europe and North America. This implied an abundance of skilled labour, which is the basic foundation for any industrial society. These conditions promised abundant bounty, but now there is a looming problem which is shared not only by northeast Asia, but also by a large part of the world. This problem is globalization.

Much has already been said here at this forum about the globalization of economic activities with particular emphasis on the expected function of free markets all over the world. Globalization with a free market system has its own problems, which has not been solved. This erupted very dramatically at the World Trade Organization's (WTO) Seattle conference in December 1999, which showed that the major problem lay in the discrepancy between the North and South. This underlines all current discussions about the world economy, the WTO and the free market.

Now I will discuss the situation in Japan. Many Japanese have pointed out that in contrast with Germany's attitude to Nazi war crimes, the Japanese feelings on its own war crimes and its aggression in mainland Asia remains ambivalent. The Japanese army, a force of roughly one million men dispersed throughout Korea, China and Southeast Asia, did tremendous damage to the material, psychological, intellectual, and cultural beings of the residents of those areas. Since that time, the Japanese Government and to some extent Japanese society's attitude regarding responsibility for the war has never been given in a clear concrete form. Japan has still not solved the problem of war responsibility.

This is one of the most important reasons why we do not have the same kind of situation like Germany. In Europe, you will see German-French reconciliation, but in Asia — Japan and Korea and China have had no such comparable reconciliation and one of the reasons, of which there are many, is Japan's attitude. This is very serious and still affects political situations in northeast Asia. The major problem of course is that the Koreas are still divided after the reunification of Germany. The severe economic and political difficulties currently facing North Korea has not helped the situation either. China has many problems of course, but politically perhaps the most serious problem is Taiwan. I am not saying that the Chinese attitude has created the Taiwan problem, but that Taiwan is the focus of different international forces that converge consequently to produce the tension that exists between Taiwan and mainland China.

In the future perhaps what we need is a regional security system, not just economic and political linkages, but a security system with the full participation of those three countries that I have already mentioned with the addition perhaps of Russia and the United States. At the moment there is no prospect for this happening and that is one of the important problems we face in the present day. Culturally speaking, the background of these economic and political problems in terms of security policy, lies in mutual trust. I have said that Japan still has not solved the question of war responsibility, which means that Japan has still not succeeded in building up mutual trust with China and Korea. This is largely due to the attitude of the Japanese and not the attitude of the Chinese or Koreans. The building up of mutual trust is something that Europeans have achieved recently.

Having trust as a foundation goes a long way to solving political problems and overcoming economic difficulties. But more important in the long term than either political or economic concerns is the question of cultural linkages between China, Japan and Korea.

However the cultural future or even the present cannot be imagined without tradition or the past. You cannot produce something out of nothing, so that all acts of creation, be they in fine arts, music, literature or poetry, are all driven by the passion of revolt against a tradition, and at the same time by the fascination of rediscovery of another. The Renaissance artists, for example, revolted against the medieval tradition in the arts, to rediscover, and consider as the basis of their creative activities, another tradition: Hellenism. At the turn of the nineteenth and the twentieth centuries, artists repudiated much of the features of the visual arts since the Renaissance, and prepared the way for new styles, borrowing from the tradition of other cultures, notably Japanese (woodcut prints), or African (Congo marks).

Now in northeast Asia there are three great spiritual, religious, and cultural belief systems shared by China, Korea and Japan for more than a thousand years. They are Confucianism, Buddhism and Daoism. There are two kinds of Daoism. One is popular Daoism, a folkloric belief system which is still alive in China, but not so much in Japan or Korea. What deeply affected the cultures of the three nations was intellectual Daoism — the philosophy of Laozi and Zhuangzi. The question is how can these old belief systems be used to create new value systems and inspire intellectual artistic creativity? What kind of traditional elements built in those systems are available need to be reexamined and revitalized?

Perhaps we should first discuss Confucianism. Confucianism is of course opposite to the very modern idea of a democratic society, being a very authoritarian and patriarchal system. Criticism of Confucianism has been very vehement at times in China, the country of its birth. But on the other hand, Confucianism was perhaps the first and most powerful belief system that emphasized the close link between politics, political behaviour and moral/ethical values without referring to a deity. There were objections that there is a Confucian heaven, but that is ancient Confucianism where heaven was somewhat like God. But in later Confucianism this heaven was depersonalized and became the symbol of constant lasting truth, but not God as a person. In that sense, Confucianism as a whole is a godless system, which has succeeded combining to some extent political behaviour, social roles and moral values.

This poses interesting possibilities for the twentieth century. Because international politics today is without moral values, there is a sharp separation between political behaviour and moral consequences. This may have begun with Machiavelli, or with the beginning of modern political science, but anyhow this separation is taken for granted, and now there are whole sets of behaviours that have nothing to do with morals. Political behaviour is calculated and indeed motivated by what the country can get out of it to the detriment of other, more spiritual concerns, not to say the needs of other nations.

This separation has brought many problems that we have not solved in the twentieth century, but which we may do so in the twenty-first. This is again not in the combination of morals and ethics that existed in the historical and social context of the fifth century B.C. in northern China, but, in other social contexts and the present-day situation concerning the relationship between ethical values and politics, so that Confucianism poses some interesting points. Confucianism was also extremely successful in its egalitarianism. Egalitarianism except for one — the emperor. All people being equal before the emperor was very much a promoted doctrine of Confucianism, so if you replace, for instance, the emperor by a system of law, then all are equal before the law. The law is made by the parliament and the parliament has replaced the king and all the people have equal rights before it. Inside the parliament the majority rules. From the nineteenth century to the present, our system of government has been characterized by what John Stuart Mill had once predicted would come to pass: the tyranny of the majority.

The tyranny of the majority, and the behaviour of the parliamentary majority in any country is not clearly defined. The problem for us here now at the end of the twentieth century is how to cope with that situation, for there is no better alternative for political authority and political power than majority party rule in a parliament. In the American constitution, the judiciary, in particular the supreme court, is independent from parliament and that implies an independence from the majority opinion of the people. In principle, the legitimization of the action of the supreme court vis-à-vis opinion of the people themselves is a moral value. So ethical values come back to that connection. A reexamination and revitalization of Confucianism should be done in the context of the twenty-first century world.

Another thing worth discussing is education. Confucianism has encouraged education, and the educational system in traditional China, at least from the Tang dynasty onwards was egalitarian in outlook. In other words, education was open to everybody who was successful in their examinations. Now that higher education is at least in principle egalitarian, so these very Confucian ideas, political ethics and emphasis on education, are very much relevant for the future.

Now on Buddhism, which consists of two schools, Mahayana Buddhism and Hinayana Buddhism. Hinayana Buddhism roughly traveled south from India to Ceylon, Thailand then on to Indonesia. Mahayana Buddhism went north by the silk road where it veered off to Tibet and Central Asia, before arriving in north China, the Korean Peninsula and thence onwards to Japan. So Chinese, Koreans, and Japanese have shared Mahayana Buddhism for centuries. One country which has experienced both Mahayana and Hinayana Buddhism was Cambodia. Mahayana Buddhism which came prior to the fourteenth century was preceded by Hinduism. Hinduism, local belief systems and the newly arrived faith gave rise to the tremendous flowering of medieval Cambodian architecture and sculpture. But Buddhist temple sculpture declined between the fourteenth to fifteenth centuries, the major reason given by scholars seemed to be the arrival of Hinayana Buddhism. Hinayana Buddhism was more fundamentalist, more pure in its beliefs, while Mahayana Buddhism was more open to compromise and the acceptance of other ideas, for instance Hinduism and other faiths in Cambodia. Buddhism in northeastern Asia today almost exclusively means Mahayana Buddhism.

Therefore, Buddhistic images of tolerance or coexistence with other belief systems, in other words a kind of philosophy of cultural pluralism has many implications that Professor Hughes has analyzed in more detail in his paper "Pluralism without Relativism in Ethics." It seems that the pluralism and coexistence of different cultural systems is one of the most important cultural problems facing us today. Mahayana Buddhism is fascinating since for a thousand years it has practised a philosophy of coexistence with other belief systems. Prepared to compromise, Mahayana Buddhism may be criticized for lack of intellectual rigour, or guiding principles. However the merits of tolerance outweigh the negative side of extreme flexibility.

Daoism is a system like Buddhism that is against violence, be it in the natural or human environment. A non-aggressive, non-violent attitude to all aspects of life is maintained at all times despite the costs this places on them. War is so destructive and so pervasive that the philosophy of non-violence has become important to many people, witness peace activists today. The first half of the twentieth century produced the most memorable philosopher of peace and practitioner of non-violence that the world has known: Mahatma Gandhi. But in my opinion, people should remember the ancient Chinese wisdom of Zhuangzi and other Daoist philosophies in the new century. If we think and act on these philosophies, then we may go some way towards our ultimate target of experiencing no war or violent act. Political decisions have often being carried out blindly, without learning the mistakes of the past, which means that we are doomed to repeat them time and again leading to destruction of human life and human culture. But still these kinds of beliefs have yet to penetrate the great masses as a whole, even in those masses where these traditions of human values have originated from — the Chinese, Japanese and Koreans.

Values in daily life are perhaps more tangible and obvious. What northeast Asian nations share is an aesthetic concern in everyday life. For example in Korea, ceramics and special lacquer technique expresses their very artistic sense in even the most mundane task of daily life. In every well-educated Chinese home, there is a piece of calligraphy hanging on the walls, indicating that Chinese characters are not only letters, ideograms, but also a means of artistic expression. Their Japanese counterparts have small gardens, flowers in all rooms, and write on fine quality paper, so that art, and therefore beauty are everyday experiences. Another important everyday value is the sense of community, be it family, village or region. But this is true of almost all human societies.

An important thing that we have in northeast Asia and shared for more than a thousand years is a writing system characterized by Chinese ideograms. Not only the Chinese, but also the Koreans and Japanese were for centuries educated and acquainted with Chinese texts; we wrote our own histories, administrative records, scholarly treatises, even our poems in classical Chinese. On the other hand, the Japanese and Koreans came to invent our alphabets (phonetic letters) to transcribe our own languages. Writing systems that consisted of a mixture of Japanese and Korean phonetic letters and Chinese ideograms became widely used in daily life, while classical Chinese long remained the language for official purposes. Although Japan was closed to foreign trade, from the early seventeenth to mid-nineteenth centuries under the Tokugawa regime, there was repeated visits by Korean government missions. Those Koreans and Japanese could not converse because of the different pronunciation, but could easily communicate via the Chinese written script. In medieval Europe, Latin was a *lingua franca*. Educated Europeans from different countries understood each other through Latin in speech and writing. In northeast Asia, classical

Chinese was the semi-*lingua franca*, a useful language for international communication, except for speech. And Classical Chinese was inseparable from Chinese classics.

The Chinese classics are like the Latin culture in Europe, it did not just belong to Italy or any other European country. Therefore these intellectual marvels are not the private property of the Chinese nation but the property of the entire world. We have borrowed from them for more than a thousand years, so it is perfectly natural to draw on their wisdom in Korea, Japan and China. Therefore a strong case can be made for studying them once again. This, alongside the other things that I have mentioned, will work towards the building up of economic, political and cultural ties in all these northeast Asian communities.

Who Is to Rescue Literature and Who Can Be Rescued by Literature?

Wang Meng

Those who hold different opinions believe China has shifted away or is still in the process of shifting away from the turbulent period of class struggle and politics holding the commanding position to a peaceful era of economic construction. People no longer, as they did in the 1970s, try to discover new signs of political life from literary works, nor do they expect literature to suggest more leading or subtle information on political or ideological trends. Literary works simply do not carry the great role of political weathervane any more. Today, no political move unfolds itself from an opera, a novel or a movie, which is simply normal. The kind of literary craze we experienced in the past was only a product of the historical conditions at that particular period of time and it is hard to repeat.

The annual average volume of literary works published in China nowadays is twenty to fifty times the total amount published in the seventeen years before the Cultural Revolution from 1949 to 1966. For example, during those seventeen years, only a dozen novels were printed each year as compared to more than five hundred these days. Every year, nearly 10,000 kinds of literary works are issued and 70 percent of them are new titles. In addition, most of the 8,000 kinds of newspapers in the country have their own literary pages or sections. The assertion that Chinese readers are turning away from literature needs concrete support to make it stand. What has changed though is that today's readers have a much wider range of materials to choose from. Mass media and audio and video art certainly have a negative effect on literature, but they also have a positive role. The rush to the bookstores for *The Besieged City* by Qian Zhongshu and *David Copperfield* by Charles Dickens, all took place after the dramas based on these works appeared on television. As for the Internet, though it makes the spread of ideas much easier and faster, it does not change the nature and function of literature. All of them may change the means of dissemination of literature, but they do not inevitably change literature itself and will not necessarily replace printed books and journals.

The audience has the right to choose the works for their own recreational and leisure life, just as critics have their right to either feel sad about or argue for these works. Pop reading materials and serious literary works are not necessarily intolerable to each other and it is very difficult for them to replace one another. Each category has its own turf. And they can coexist and even learn from one another. Of course it should be admitted that there are clashes. Critics naturally have the responsibility to try to persuade readers to pick up the works of elite writers but it does them no harm to try to understand the pluralism of the varieties and functions of literary works. When the nation is in difficulty, often it is a highly creative time for poets. Great authors and spiritual masters like Lu Xun existed only given the historical situation on the eve of the total collapse of the old China. It is hard to imagine that any other writer today emerging as a spiritual leader of the public and trying to imitate the former. Writer-turned spiritual leaders will simply not produce the same kind of effect. What is more, whether people in China today badly want to have some kind of writer to channel their path is a big question. Even if there is a great writer, it would be a cloned Lu Xun. Perhaps what is needed today are intelligent writers who can be friends of the public, more thoughtful and reasonable rather than brave mobilizers with strong voices and explosive characters.

Personally I am basically in agreement with the latter two kinds of opinions. At the same time, I believe anxiety, criticism, blame and lamentation help people realize the existence of the loss of values and the impoverishment of people's cultural life as well as the need for people to shake off ignorance while freeing themselves from economic poverty, at a time when the fabric of society is changing and the economy is going through speedy development. Opinions of blame also help us to seriously come to see and learn from lessons of history so that everybody will work to create an even better and sounder cultural eco-environment. Our basic lessons are: only when there is enough room for cultural activities and only when people have a more open attitude, can there be creation of new works that live up to the great traditions of Chinese literature.

Criticism and blame also lead writers to think and discover their own (cultural and academic) weaknesses and inadequacies, and draw up higher demands for them. The revitalization and fate of literature are directly related to writers but also have something to do with the standard of publishing, editing, distribution, mass media, acceptance and leadership. As we enter the twenty-first century, we should learn from the very basics.

The development of literature always goes with political and economic pressures. It is hard to imagine that writers could easily and pleasantly be raised and be put high in the limelight with everything going peacefully and still produce great works at the same time.

We can say that literature needs outside redemption, almsgiving and attention. That literature needs the social power of authority to clear the way for its development, to clear the light literature and purify the public media. We can also say that literature requires qualified people at large in the society, requires poetizing circumstances and that the policy is a decisive factor for literature developing and imagining that the creative environment be idealized. Instead, we had better say that Chinese literature needs more effort from itself, needs more learning, needs making up the missed lessons, and that the writers themselves need improvement of their diathesis. It is better to exert your utmost strength in your creative writings than complaining all day. It is not too late to make proclamations and to complain before you give something real to the readers.

In fact, the history of literature of ancient times as well as today proves that no great works can be written in ideal circumstances. Of course this does not mean that people, especially the authorities, should build obstacles and create tribulation for writers. With the growth of the economy, conditions for the greater development of cultural and educational undertakings will also present themselves. I do not mean to suggest that the economic growth is a panacea for everything.

In China, literature is unlikely to once again become the focus of social life but neither will it become totally marginal. China is a country with long literary traditions. It is a tradition for Chinese people including both ordinary citizens and leaders to pay great attention to the social functions of literature — sometimes they pay too much attention instead of overlooking them. Those who hold the view that China will be changed into a commercialized country only partially know the real situation.

Before I continue, I must reiterate that what Chinese people can get nowadays in their daily life is still limited. But even in their pursuit of reality nowadays, I think Chinese people can manage to preserve a piece of spiritual land for themselves and to find the spiritual resources, the possibility of enriching their humanity in their search and their study of literature, philosophy, religion and in the cultural accumulation. In the meantime, Chinese people may have noticed their spiritual hunger during this period of social change and are trying to do something to satisfy it with literature. On the other hand, in the world of today, which has become more commercialized, more technical, more digital and more accurate, it is literature that gives us some warmth, some enthusiasm, some secrecy, some dreams, something romantic, something beautiful, something uncertain and something plastic.

It is also literature that gives us some remembrance of the remote antiquity of the human race in its childhood. It could give those living on earth and still in their caves with limited outlook some experience of flying, zero gravity, craziness and dizziness, some experience of nobleness, yearning, heroism and narcissism even if that could be laughed at. It is like something in other fields. People may be disappointed, may be critical about everything, but amidst ridicule and blame, Chinese literature will continue to develop and gain new vitality in the new millennium.

Creation of Wealth Using Knowledge Systems in the New Millennium

Paul Kan Man-lok

On a company's balance sheet, you will not find knowledge listed. Knowledge carries no value. If you try to discuss it with accountants — I don't know whether we have any accountants here — they will argue that it is impossible to put a value on knowledge, and it is something that no one can catch or value properly. There is a great resistance to change and this is actually discussed in the book that I have given out today. It was published on 1 January 2000 and so it will make a very good souvenir in another hundred years' time.

A funny phenomenon arises from the fact that nobody puts any value on knowledge. If you talk to an accountant, he will argue that knowledge has no value, so you can give him the following example: you're working for an accounting firm with a hundred years of experience when suddenly one of the young accountants resigns and sets up office next door. He buys new premises, computers, new typewriters and new furniture. And so his balance sheet will carry a value of something like ten million dollars. But when you look at the balance sheet of the hundred-year-old accountancy firm, its balance sheet is more or less nothing — because the furniture or equipment has been written off. If I'm a new client, looking at the balance sheet of the company, I'm going to use the service of the new company since he has assets of ten million dollars! But the experienced company has no assets. Their balance sheet is zero and the accountant will find it very peculiar. As an auditor, he keeps asking people what is the most valuable asset, and they reply: knowledge. When it comes to his own territory he doesn't know what to do about it.

We all know it's wrong. I can tell you why and I'm sure you know why: because the most valuable asset in that company are the clients. The hundred-year-old accountancy firm has handled 100,000 cases and performed all sorts of accounting practices. Clients have already paid for their service. The cost is being paid for by the clients. So it never appears on the balance sheet, despite the firm's extensive knowledge on how to handle the accounts of oil companies, supermarkets, department stores, and all sorts of various businesses. They acquire a lot of knowledge, but this is not listed on the balance sheet. So in the new millennium, people are starting to realize that knowledge is actually worth a lot of money, for it has been invested over a long time. The reason why we are waking up to this fact is because of the development of computer software.

In the 1970s, IBM decided to unbundle its computer hardware and software because they wanted to lower the price of each of these items. Then IBM produced the basic help that led to the creation of Microsoft MS-DOS; the company thought that was a smart move. But actually it was not because Microsoft now has a market capitalization much bigger than that of IBM. People now realize that knowledge, or intellectual property, carries a value much higher than its counterpart, the physical part of the business.

There are actually two components in the value of anything: the physical part of the thing and the knowledge part. You look at a building and you say, "that building is worth ten million dollars." But the bricks are not worth that much money — it's the architectural fee, and the engineering fee involved in its construction. The construction costs of the building do not just include the bricks and mortar, but a vast amount of intellectual endeavour. The accountants are generous in allowing the capitalization of architectural fees as part of the building's construction cost. So what happened was, five hundred years ago, when accountancy was first invented, it was for the old economy. You look at gold: the value of gold includes all the excavation costs. It's not just the minerals, not the sand. You look at the microchip: it cost something like 12 US dollars per chip. It's sand. It's silicon. Just pick it up and see. It's the intellectual properties inside it that make it valuable.

It is the same for human beings. If you did not have a brain, or if you were dead, you probably would not sell for 5 dollars per kg as meat. It's because you have a brain, because you have intellectual capabilities, and that is why you are being paid 10,000 or 100,000 or one million dollars a month. People complain, "Computer software is so expensive." I own computer software. I'm also software. I'm also physical. I'm also intellectual.

The carpenter will say, "this table, this desk, the wood alone is worth five dollars; but my design, my workmanship, is worth one thousand dollars." So I have two components also. The physical part of anything has a limit. You build this table. The table can sit, say, a maximum of ten people or twenty people. It has a capacity. In this room, you can put a hundred people maximum; but the intellectual part has no limit. The maximum capacity of any intellectual or knowledge part of the component — you can sell so many times — is as big as the market and it will be as big as the size of the market it is building.

People tend to go on historical figures: how big is the market? When I first developed a pager and discussed it with someone I had just met, this person said, "How many you have sold?" I said, "Well, I have not sold any." "So it has no market," he replied. It's funny the way people think: because you've never done it before, it therefore has no market.

It's just like the story of the two salesmen traveling across the Pacific Ocean. The ship sinks and they swim to a small island. One of them says, "Oh my god," and sends a telex home saying "there's no market, none of the local Indians wear shoes." The other saleman sends a telex back saying "Oh my god, I can capture a hundred percent of the market — nobody wears shoes." So headquarters get two messages: one message says there is no market, while the other says there is a huge market.

So, in the future, people will realize that intellectual property will have a market the size that it is going to build, because in theory everybody has and can use that intellectual property. But if you use the physical part, it has a limit. If this is a building, if this is gold, it has a limit. The physical part of the gold has a limit. But if you talk about intellectual property, or how to mine gold, you can resell it many times. So all you have to do is to separate the two parts and try to resell the intellectual part. And this is wealth. In the past, I can sell five copies of a book. This is just the cost of the paper. But if I separate the physical and the intellectual value, sell the paper with the book, and sell the intellectual property on the World Wide Web, I have as large a market as the number of people accessing the web. People who are willing to pay for it can download it — at the moment, unfortunately, Net culture is free of charge — you can sell it so many times. In short, we need a new system of accounting to reflect the true value of modern knowledge assets if we want to create wealth using knowledge systems in the new millennium.

Unfortunately people still use money as the primary score or indication of success. So people want to get rich. It is an unfortunate value in the new millennium. In the new millennium, on the Net, it is still the only single measurement of success. People tend to say, "It is the fault of the media." On the front page of newspapers and magazines, it's who makes the most money. You don't remember who's the president but you will remember the lucky fellow who reaches millionaire status. You won't remember what some of the sportsmen have done, but you will know how much money he has made. You don't remember his Olympic records, but you will remember the athlete who had made a lot of money. You remember the golfer who won ten million dollars. You tend to remember people by how much money they earn.

As youngsters brought up in the new millennium, you will always want to get rich quick. And you are spoiled because you have the Net. Apart from being born with a silver spoon in your mouth, you are born with a mouse in your hand. One click and you'll have everything. Just one click. In small families, the children are often spoiled. Their parents will spend time going around trying to buy things for the young kids, spending a lot of time making phone calls, going around town on their behalf, so the children will tend to take for granted things they want. One click away and we can compare all manner of things on our computers. If you want to know where to find the cheapest, the lowest-price-best-performance item, you can do it with one click of the mouse. People, computer programmes, software, websites, whatever — the best bargains can be had very easily. So suddenly if you don't have the help of the Internet, you don't know what to do. You are starting to lose your power of contrast, of comparison. If somebody gives you a series of random numbers, you cannot rank them. Try to rank them in sequence. It's impossible because you are losing that power. Now I find a lot of youngsters who are not capable of using their minds to add up a few simple numbers.

A person working for me, who has a doctorate from Harvard, used a computer to add up something like ten different numbers, each one with five digits, and he ended up with an eight digit number. I said, "You can't be right because ten times five digits has a maximum of six digits. It can't be eight digits. So something's wrong." He said, "The computer gives me the right answer." I said, "No, because you have put in the wrong numbers."

"It's not that the computer that has to be right," I said, "It's you who put in something wrong." He said, "How come you know? You don't have the computer." I said, "Look at ten numbers with five digits. It's impossible to have eight digits. Simple."

He said, "Who ever taught you that? Nobody taught me that. They never taught this at Harvard." I said, "you don't need to learn this at Harvard. It's simple arithmetic."

He said, "No, no, no. It's got to be right." He put them in again. Wrong

again. He had used seven digits. I said, "you've put in something wrong."
So simple. So people are losing that power to do it mentally. They don't
know what their brains are for. They just use their fingers, on the web, on
the Internet.

As we have to talk about humanity and culture in the new millennium,
I think I'd rather talk more on the effect of the digital economy and the
analogy economy. And this is not all; culture is undergoing tremendous
changes. People are spoiled. Youngsters are spoiled. They are not so
healthy because they are spending huge slabs of time sitting hunched over
peering at a screen. They have problems in the fingers and the hands —
from using the mouse too much — and they have become very direct. They
become very outspoken because they talk to the screen. They don't respond to facial expressions and body language. If you interact physically
with a person, if you anger him, he may chop you, take out a knife and chop
you, because he is so angry. But if you talk on the screen, he's a thousand
miles away. You won't know if he is angry or not. You don't care because
he cannot reach out and touch you. But we are bringing up people who
don't realize that if you do something drastic, you'll get a certain reaction.
You do it on the screen, and nobody notices. You don't care. We are
bringing up a very direct younger generation.

This is both good and bad. We are building a web on the Internet. It is
about "geo-relationship." We're investing in the Silicon Valley, installing
a system developed by a professor at UCLA. He's also a psychiatrist. He
says that on the Web, we can have a psychiatrist talking to the patient and
then they try to compare human interaction and interaction between patient
and psychiatrist on the screen. He says he needs one or two fewer sessions
to get to the same point. It will take the patient two or fewer sessions on the
web to reveal that he actually feels he is underpaid, not that the boss is
treating him badly. When he goes and sees a psychiatrist in person, he says
that his boss treats him badly. When he talks to the computer, it is very easy
for him to say that he is underpaid. So the real problem is that he is
underpaid, not that his boss doesn't treat him well. But in person, he is shy.
He has an ego problem. He doesn't want to tell the psychiatrist he is
underpaid. So instead of saying this he says "I am being poorly treated. I
have to work overtime. I have to do this and have to do that." But when he
talks to the computer, he is not embarrassed to say, "I'm underpaid." He
doesn't care. The computer actually gives you an opportunity to be more
direct.

So interpersonal relationships begin to change. In the old days, people were subtler, more graceful. You brush your teeth before you talk to someone. But now, when you get up in the morning, you don't have to comb your hair. You don't wash your face. You're going to talk to the computer! The computer doesn't care. The computer won't say, "You have bad breath." So the way we live is undergoing a fundamental change. Very soon people will say to you, "How come you don't brush your teeth?" "Oh no, no, nobody taught me how to brush my teeth. I get up and then talk to the computer. And the computer doesn't care." So we have to develop programmes such as "Have you brushed your teeth first"? Otherwise we'll be breeding a new generation who are unaccustomed to the real world.

Then there is another very dangerous trend — to get rich quick. I have problems finding staff. People are not willing to work unless you give them some stock options because they all want to get rich quick. I have youngsters coming to me — I try to encourage young talent — who say "I have this concept of a company. I ask my professor and he says that this idea is worth 15 million US dollars! Please give me ten million to invest in this project."

And I say, "What have you done?" He says, "I have this concept."

I reply, "Do you have a business plan?" "No I don't have a business plan."

I say, "Can you go and do one first?" He says, "How do I write one?"

I say, "you go and learn how to do a business plan, I cannot do it for you."

A short while later he returns with something that looks like a business plan, but a plan that won't produce a profit. So I say, "You don't have any profits. How can you do any evaluation?" He says, "Oh we don't need profits. We just need the concept."

So I say "Have you done a prototype?" He says, "I don't know how to do a prototype."

"You don't have a prototype, how can it be? It seems that all you have is a concept."

He says, "How can I produce a prototype? I have to hire someone."

I say to him: "You don't know how to do a prototype."

I say, "All entrepreneurs start off small. You go and do it somewhere, rent a small room, or do it in your backyard — but you have to come up with something first."

They just want to get rich quick, without trying to figure out how to do it, and they are not even willing to spend time on making a prototype. They just want the "get rich" part without the "hardship" part.

We're already breeding these people because they often see on the television and in the newspapers that people get rich quick. A long time ago I asked a young man why everybody wants things to happen so quickly. He said, "Actually, it's the television. Because most people have a television now and everything happens very quickly on it." In a half-an-hour programme, or a one-hour programme, you can see someone born, grow up, get an education, find a job, get married, have children, get rich. It all happens in half an hour. So if somebody comes to me and works for one month and hasn't either been promoted or been given a raise in that time, then it's too long.

But this is what is happening to our young students today. They need something like six years for primary education, three years for kindergarten, another five to six years for secondary education and another three to four years for university education. They join your company for one month and then they want to get promoted! They cannot wait even two months. They want to get rich today or yesterday.

So I think it's part of the education system. I think the schools or the universities have to do something. You have to tell them "You have three years of education now. So in the real world, when you get a job, you'll have to work somewhere for a minimum of four years to get a good grounding in society. Otherwise, you are not going to get rich."

Bill Gates didn't arrive yesterday. Bill Gates has had a company for more than twenty years now. But most people just want to say, "I want to be Bill Gates but I don't want to go through what Bill Gates has gone through."

You also need to have a good family. People want to be as rich as Richard Li, but they don't have Li Ka Shing as their father. In the Buddhist world, you have to work hard this life, so that next life you'll be born into a very good family. We're talking about one's current lifetime, not just four months or four years. So you have to work hard in this life, in order to be born into a good family in the next life. I think human values will change very quickly. And when it does we have to watch out very carefully.

The Cultural Identity of Hong Kong in the New Millennium

Ambrose Y. C. King

The cultural identity of Hong Kong is inevitably linked to its political and economic identities. At the profoundest level, it is these two components that form the constitutional elements of its cultural makeup. It is the imbalance between them that makes Hong Kong's cultural identity so complex.

Hong Kong's Multi-layered Identity

Hong Kong's political identity was forged when the British Empire's gunboat diplomacy forced the Qing court to sign the Treaty of Nanjing in 1842, ceding Hong Kong, which was thereafter reduced to the status of a British colony, a totally dependent entity. Since the 1970s, and especially in the 1990s, the British Government consciously carried out a policy of decolonization, including limited democratization, which saw the emergence of a "political society" for the first time. However with Britain's departure after the Handover in 1997, Hong Kong became a Special Administrative Region of China within the framework of "One Country, Two Systems." Although it was "Hong Kong people governing Hong Kong with a high degree of autonomy," Hong Kong was still a dependent entity politically. This new political identity has not yet been fully embraced by the Hong Kong polity — rather it is still evolving and taking shape.

As for its economic identity, Henry Pottinger, the second governor of Hong Kong, wanted the colony to become a commercial port and a transit point for its maritime trade with China. Hong Kong's commercial development was intrinsically connected with its colonial status till the 1970s when geo-economic factors saw Hong Kong gradually become an international city, and after the 1980s, a world-class financial centre. Hong Kong is an important link in international capitalism, a burgeoning industrial region that has emerged as one of the "four little dragons" of East Asia. It is worth mentioning that long before 1997, the Chinese had surpassed the British as dominant players in the local economy. Hong Kong also enjoys the position of being the capital of the "overseas Chinese."

Hong Kong's new economic status has not only meant that any lingering sense of colonialism has been shaken off, it also enabled Hong Kong to assist in China's economic development once it launched its Open Door policy and the Four Modernizations in 1978. So for a time, Hong Kong's capitalists and cultural producers developed a "northern imagination" and the idea of a "Greater Hong Kong." Indeed the political identity of Hong Kong as a dependent entity is at odds with its economic entity which is seen as central to the global financial structure. The average income of Hong Kong people far exceeds that of the mainland Chinese and is higher than the average annual income of Britain. Deng Xiaoping's policy of "One Country, Two Systems" for Hong Kong's return to China was a pragmatic and creative solution. It can be said that "one country" is to define Hong Kong's political identity, while "two systems" is to define its economic identity. It is true that this policy has intrinsic contradictions, but it does provide space for reconciling the conflict between them.

Hong Kong Is No Longer Peripheral

As mentioned previously, the political and economic identities of Hong Kong are fundamental to its cultural identity. But this identity also has deeper cultural and ethnic roots. For the last 150 years, Hong Kong has been on the periphery of both the Chinese motherland and the British Empire, and been isolated from the great traditions of both China and Britain. It had no part in the major cultural changes that took place in those two countries over the last one hundred years (both the New Culture Movement in China and one hundred years of democratic development in England completely bypassed Hong Kong).

Such was the case that when Lu Xun came to Hong Kong around 1927, he only stayed for three days and heaped scorn on the city in his essay "Some Brief Remarks on Hong Kong." Many scholars after him, whether they came from the Mainland, Taiwan or elsewhere, generally thought little of Hong Kong culture: "What is there to say about it? " What they actually meant was "high-brow" culture.

Looking at it from another angle, Hong Kong was destined to be a place where Chinese and Western civilization blurred and intermingled. During his thirty years in Hong Kong, the missionary-translator James

Legge translated the *Four Books* and *Five Classics*. This symbolically explains Hong Kong's characteristic Chinese-Western mix. As a matter of fact, at the end of the twentieth century, Hong Kong is the most Western and most modern of all Chinese communities. It may well be argued that its highly sophisticated modern institutions (especially the legal and administrative systems) are why Hong Kong is an international city of the first order and provided the foundation for it to become a true metropolis during the current wave of globalization. For a long time, Hong Kong has been the forerunner of modernization in the Chinese world, so by the time China began to pursue the Four Modernizations, culture in Hong Kong enjoyed a more prestigious status in comparison. In a certain sense, Hong Kong acted as an indictor of cultural modernization. This is why there has been a cultural discourse on "the periphery as the centre" because, from modernization's point of view, Hong Kong is no longer a periphery.

Against this background, the idea of "cultural China," which has gained wide acceptance in Chinese academic circles in recent years, became particularly significant. Moreover, the concept that "the periphery as the centre" is not just because Hong Kong is more modern than other Chinese communities, it is also because from 1949 onwards, and especially during the Great Cultural Revolution, Chinese culture has been systematically attacked and damaged in mainland China. Central Plains culture no longer had its charismatic appeal. If we understand it this way, this concept makes a lot of sense.

Hong Kong's change of sovereignty has led to many new explorations and reconstructions of Hong Kong's historical memories and traditions in the media, giving rise to many different Hong Kong stories. You could see it as Hong Kong's glorious return to the motherland after its seizure and repression by a colonial power, a story that has both romance and tragedy. You could also see it as how a small fishing village became a great international city — quite an amazing feat. Both these stories are real and imagined. Indeed, the "real" Hong Kong story cannot be told without employing some historical imagination. So when you talk of Hong Kong today, you have to reconstruct and reinterpret its past. Looking back, we could argue that three powerful historical forces have shaped Hong Kong over the last 150 years: capitalism (economic force), colonialism (political force) and modernity (cultural force). These three forces have determined the course of Hong Kong's development and they have had both good and bad effects. They are not rigidly bound together, but Hong Kong's historical experiences have meant that they cannot entirely be separated. This has produced the complexity and contradictions in Hong Kong's identity.

Regardless whether it is a colonial or an international city, it is difficult for Hong Kong to become a true world city, since over 97 percent of its inhabitants are Chinese. Naturally enough it is this racial composition that forms the basis to Hong Kong's cultural identity. Hong Kong, unlike other world cities that built on multiculturalism and a high degree of hybridization, has a cultural duality. Although a mixed society to a certain degree, Hong Kong consists essentially of two racial groups — Chinese and European. There is a "double consciousness" since Hong Kong people consider themselves Western as well as Chinese (or Hong Kongers). Since Chinese make up the most of the population, the majority identify with Chinese culture. However, this does not make the identity of Hong Kong Chinese uncomplicated or straightforward. The surveys conducted by Lau Siu-kai from the Sociology Department of The Chinese University of Hong Kong, in 1988 and 1994 respectively, showed that 36.5 percent and 56.5 percent of Hong Kong Chinese consider themselves Hong Kongers and 28.8 percent and 38.2 percent consider themselves to be Chinese. Thus it can be seen that Hong Kong Chinese have a double identity as both Hong Kongers and Chinese. I believe that this separated identity is related to political differences rather than a differences in culture, since the 1985 survey showed that 60.5 percent of respondents agreed or strongly agreed that Chinese culture is the best in the world, and 78.6 percent of people say that they are proud to be Chinese. In the 1994 survey, it was found that 92.9 percent of Hong Kong people agreed that in present-day Hong Kong, traditional Chinese values (such as loyalty, filial piety, benevolence and righteousness) should still be respected. It is apparent from these surveys that the Hong Kong Chinese consider themselves Hong Kongers only in respect to their political identity.

Hong Kong Positioning Itself Dialectically between the Global and the Local

The identity of Hong Kong Chinese only became an issue because of the change of sovereignty in 1997. On the collective level, its cultural identity has become a crucial factor in the implementation of "One Country, Two Systems." As mentioned above, Hong Kong's cultural identity is inextricably entwined with its economic and political identity. In its 150-year history, it has had historical memories, historical forgetfulness, and historical imagination; there has also been colonization and decolonization, de-sinocization and re-sinocization.

Modern Hong Kong finds itself in a new century, and in addition to being assigned a new political identity as a Special Administrative Region of China, it also faces an unprecedented tide of globalization. However globalization is not a recent phenomenon, it first occurred in the early twentieth century after the First World War. But this time, globalization has forged ahead at breakneck speed due to the information technology revolution. Hong Kong will strengthen its economic identity as an international city, and this will form the core of the its new cultural identity.

Where does Hong Kong's future lie? As a Hongkonger living in Hong Kong, I hold the view that it lies in positioning itself as an international city and it must use all its strength to hold onto this position. As an international city, Hong Kong's new cultural identity has to be pluralistic, and it also has to accept the new set of global ethics and values that have emerged in recent years, like the recognition of human rights and the protection of the environment. This should not be construed as a value conflict between Chinese and Western. We have already spent one hundred years arguing about what is "Chinese" and what is "Western." Hong Kong should move beyond the Chinese versus Western mindset and break through the centre/periphery construct. Hong Kong should position itself dialectically within these two alternatives.

The Centrality of Hong Kong Culture

The Club of Rome published a book in 1991 called *The First Global Revolution.* In it they wrote: "It is difficult to imagine creating a world society if there is nothing in common, or exclusive of other cultural values. It is only with common values that humanity will be able to confront challenges together and have the moral force to change the world." In fact, from the perspective of Chinese and Western values, some have already become world values. This clearly means that when humankind is inclusive of the diversity and pluralism in each other's cultures, global society can become a reality. Even more importantly, they understood that the global and local could exist together at the same time. A global society is not a homogenous mass, but pluralistic in nature, and it is only through pluralism that we can boldly seek a system of global ethics.

Hong Kong has to face the future, and it cannot reject globalization. Does this mean that it will lose its identity in the process? The answer is no.

Hong Kong still has its own cultural identity, and its own place in the world. Hong Kong exists on this planet as a "locale," and naturally it should have its own global-local cultural mix. The main cultural resources of Hong Kong come from Chinese traditions and Hong Kong's cultural subjectivity is destined to have Chinese culture as its cornerstone. And only when Hong Kong firmly established its own cultural subjectivity will it cast off its cultural marginality forever and become a truly modern Chinese metropolis.

As Hong Kong was welcoming in the millennium, I saw a lantern of Santa Claus sitting on the back of a gigantic dragon in Victoria Harbour — doesn't this symbolize the relationship between local and global?

Whose Millennium Is It Anyway? Beauty, Truth and Justice at the Fin-de-Siècle

Linda Nochlin

In a recent article in the *New York Times* headed "A Carnival of Derision to Greet the Princes of Global Trade," (*New York Times*, Saturday, 8 January 2000) a protester against the World Trade Organization (WTO), one Alli Starr, a dancer in the radical group Art and Revolution, is reported to have declared "the WTO responds to the needs and interests of the very rich and corporations, but it doesn't respond to the needs of the environment, labour, the poor, women or indigenous people." Now no matter what you feel about the WTO, this is obviously, rightly or wrongly, a heartfelt criticism, something that came from deep within. I might say that I have had somewhat the same reaction to the over-hyped celebrations constructed around the new millennium. In short, I feel the same way about the millennium.

First of all I have to ask: whose millennium is it anyway? For Islam the so-called millennium is the year 1421 in North America; the Jewish calendar marks the year as 5760; for Buddhists who calculate the calendar differently in different parts of the world, this is 2543, using the year 543 B.C.E as the basis. On the Chinese Calendar evidently, the year 2000 is the year 4697, the year of the golden dragon, although some websites I consulted maintained that it's the 4698th Chinese year. The Christian calendar itself has gone through some alteration, since the not completely authenticated birthday of its founding figure. Then who is this "we" who is celebrating what in the most literal sense, if not entirely accurately, is called the 2000th birthday of one Jesus Christ — certainly not the majority of those living on this earth for whom the Christian calendar is after all a mere convenience? Certainly not the vast multitude of Jews, Muslims, Buddhists, Hindus and others who populate this earth. And what does such a celebration of Western, white, mostly male cultural values mean for the rest of us? Where is the voice, the overwhelmingly larger voice, of the Others in this post-colonial narrative? In short, to borrow the words of novelist of Joyce Carol Oates, writing on the Op-Ed page of the *New York Times* ten days before the major date of 2000, and I quote "Since the calendar numeral 2000 A.D. has little intrinsic meaning to the majority of the world's people, many of whose traditions predate the Christian era, this elevation of the Western/Christian/Caucasian millennium is embarrassingly chauvinistic." She goes on to assert that millenarian fantasies spring from what she aptly calls "the fallacy of the round number." "You understand that nothing much can happen in A.D. 999 or A.D. 1999 but a frenzy comes over you to believe that *something must happen* in A.D.1000 (but what did?) and in A.D. 2000."

Now I have deliberately chosen to focus on one of the outsider groups mentioned by that protester Alli Starr: Women. Half of the world's population to be sure, and certainly a group that has made a great deal of progress in recent years, at least in part due to the International Women's Movement, but still a group on the fringes of the cultural action in many cases. Because this occasion would seem to call for some resounding and dignified generalizations, some grandiose universals about art and its past, present and future, I have chosen the most grandiose categories possible: Beauty, Truth and Justice — nothing could be grander or more universal than these. Yet, as I have no more faith in universals than I have in millennia, I have decided to resort to the mode of allegory for my presentation.

Hovering between deconstruction and dialectics, as cultural critic Gail Day has recently put it, the allegorical mode has the virtue of arbitrariness, the breaking of sign from reference and signifier from signified. (Day, 1999:103–18) It depends for its work on such concepts as discontinuity, rupture, threshold limits and transformation. (Douglas Crimp, cited in Day, 1999:106) and rejects "the unities of historicist thought as tradition, influence, development, source and origin." (*ibid.*) What can Beauty, Truth and Justice mean for women, women artists specifically, at the millennium? In choosing the allegorical mode for my presentation and such traditionally unifying, timeless grounding concepts as Beauty, Truth and Justice, I am in no sense attempting to elevate these women's projects by asserting some sort of totalizing, global, universal value to their achievement. On the contrary, I will be using the actual work of contemporary women artists, two living, and one recently dead, to question the viability, the value claims and the very possibility of these traditional universals at our fin-de-siècle. I will in a sense, be deconstructing these concepts by means of extremely concrete examples from specific careers at a particular moment in history, conceiving my narrative as an interchange between art object and creative process, viewer and viewed. My talk is to be dedicated to three very different women artists: Joan Mitchell, an American who died a few years ago, Jenny Saville, a young British artist who I think has just reached the age of thirty, and Rachel Whiteread, a somewhat older British artist. They are by no means "representative" and they are of course the products of the same Western culture that has produced the millennium. But their work illustrates, powerfully I believe, alternatives to and interventions against, that all-too-global culture which threatens to sweep us all up in its smothering, mindless, mass-produced embrace.

For my example of beauty, I have chosen the work of the abstract artist, Joan Mitchell. It is not, however, beauty alone I wish to address in this case, but the more complex issue of the intersection of rage and beauty in the work of a major woman artist of the second half of the twentieth century.

Rage, violence, and anger have often been deployed as heuristic keys in interpreting the work of Joan Mitchell, especially the early work like *To the Harbourmaster* of 1957 and *Untitled* of 1958. For example, Judith Bernstock, in her 1988 catalogue of a major retrospective of Mitchell's work ties *To the Harbourmaster* to the poem by Frank O'Hara from which the artist derived her title, explicitly to the lines using the symbolism of water as the element of chaos, creation and destruction. Bernstock continues her interpretation of the work by taking account of Gaston Bachelard's theory that "violent water traditionally appears as male and malevolent and is given the psychological features of anger in poetry." She goes on to maintain that both Mitchell's "frenzied painting" and O'Hara's poem "evoke a fearful water with invincible form ('metallic coils' and 'terrible channels'), and voice-like anger, a destructive force threatening internal and external chaos." Bernstock then inserts a biographical reference: "The painting suggests the anger involved in the inevitable frustration of one's ambivalent attempt to break away from familial bonds" and finally concludes with an analysis of the formal elements involved in evoking the menacing mood of the poem: "…the cacophonous frenzy of short, criss-crossing strokes of intense colour … the agitation heightened as lyrical arm-long sweeps across the top of the canvas press down forcefully, even oppressively, on the ceaseless turbulence below." (Bernstock, 1988:47–51)

Of *Rock Bottom,* a work of 1960–61, Mitchell herself maintains: "It's a very violent painting, and you might say sea, rocks…" (Mitchell cited in

Bernstock, 1988:57) Of the whole group of canvases created from 1960 to 1962, like *Flying Dutchman, Plus ou Moins, Frémicourt* and *Cous-Cous*, the artist asserts: [these are] "very violent and angry paintings" and adds that by 1964 she was "trying to get out of a violent phase and into something else." (Mitchell cited in Bernstock, 1988:60) This "something else" was a series of sombre paintings Mitchell created in 1964, works which she called "my black paintings — although there's no black in any of them." (Mitchell cited in *Joan Mitchell:* "...my black paintings ...,")[1] In their thick, clotted paint application and sombre pigmentation, they constitute a break from the intensely coloured, energetic all-over style of her earlier production. They also seem to mark an end to the self-styled "violent" phase of Mitchell's work and a transition to a different sort of expressive abstraction.

Issues of intentionality aside, what do we mean by violence, rage and anger in terms of its inscription in the work of art? How do such emotions get into the work? How are they read out of it by the work's interpreter?

In earlier art, when anger or violence is the actual subject of the work itself, as it is in Antonio Canova's *Hercules and Licas*, the task of interpretation may seem easier, the emotion itself unambiguously present, even transparent, despite the smooth surfaces and neo-classical *stille grosse* of Canova's style. Yet even here, in the *Hercules and Licas,* with its furious hero and horrified victim, or in an image like Cézanne's convulsive image of hands-on murder, *Strangled Woman*, certain problems of interpretation arise: is Cézanne's painting a more effective representation of rage than Canova's sculpture simply because we can read a coded message of violence directly from the formal structure of the work: from its exaggerated diagonal composition, its agitated brushwork, its distorted figure-style? Clearly, the problem of just what constitutes and hence is read as rage — or in fact, any specific emotion in art — becomes both more and less complicated when the painting is abstract, that is to say, without an explicit subject, to provide a basis for interpretation. In the case of Abstract Expressionist work like Mitchell's, even the titles may prove to be deceptive or irrelevant, created for the most part, after the fact. The task of interpretation is both an exhilarating and a daunting one, the canvases functioning as so many giant Rorschach tests with ontological, or at the very least, epistemological pretensions. Biography may loom large in such cases because of the very *absence* of a recognizable subject matter in abstract works. The gesture seems to constitute a direct link to the psyche of the artist without even an apple or a jug to mediate the emotional velocity of the feeling in question.

Yet despite the unreliability of biography as an explanation of the work of art, it cannot be altogether avoided, although it certainly must be severed from the naïve notion of direct causality: "Mitchell was sad because of the death of her father so she made dark paintings." The role of rage in the psychic structure of the artist and her production is a daunting one: anger may be repressed, it may be "expressed" in a variety of ways; it may be, even, transformed into its opposite, into a pictorial construction which suggests to the viewer calm, joy, elegance. In any case, its role is always a mediated one.

But I have been talking about rage and its expression in abstract painting in general terms. Now I want to look at rage and gender: *gendered* rage. For Mitchell, of course, was a *woman* abstract painter, even though, quite understandably, she did not want to be thought of as such when she painted the works I have been talking about. Indeed, there is an apposite story about Mitchell told by Elaine de Kooning, in 1971 about the term, "women artists." "I was talking to Joan Mitchell at a party ten years ago when a man came up to us and said, 'What do you women artists think...'Joan grabbed my arm and said, 'Elaine, let's get the hell out of here.'" (Elaine de Kooning and Rosalyn Drexler, 1973:56) Mitchell was fleeing what at the time was a demeaning categorization: femininity. Like other ambitious young abstractionists in the 1950s and 1960s who happened to be women she wanted to be thought of as "one of the boys." As far as her work was concerned. I well remember, in the same period, being told several times by men who meant it as a compliment: "You think like a man." and feeling both pleased and angry about it. After all, nobody wanted to be told they "thought like a woman" ! What was meant by such a double edged compliment was of course: "You can *really* think" (how surprising!) with the underlying presupposition that only men could really think: that true thought was by definition masculine. If Mitchell didn't want to be categorized as a woman painter, it was because she wanted to be a *real* painter, by definition, masculine — a real abstract painter, someone with balls and guts, a risk-taker and ambitious.

Mitchell was one of many women at the time, trying to make it in a man's world, on men's terms, even if they were not acknowledged as such. These women included painters, writers, musicians and academics. It seems to me, then, important to examine not merely how rage may be said to get into painting or sculpture, but how it got into women. In order to do so, I will have to deal, not so much with biography, but with the more general conditions obtaining for the production and valuing of women's work in the 1950s and 1960s.

Here, I think it is useful to look at a much-used comparison between two photographs — and then a third. The first of course is the famous Jackson Pollock caught in the dance-like throes of sublime inspiration, captured by Hans Namath. It is a dynamic icon of the transcendent authority of (male) Abstract Expressionist creation. The second image, a 1951 photograph by Cecil Beaton of a fashion model posing in front of a Jackson Pollock painting, created for *Vogue* has been used to stand for, to put it bluntly, the corruption of the ideal; the transformation, inevitable in late capitalist society, of creative authenticity — a momentary illusion, at best — into commodity.[2]

As is usual in such visual demonstrations of social corruption — and one might think of George Grosz or Otto Dix's trenchant satires after World War I, or later, those of Kitaj — it is the bodies of women, inert, passive, lavishly bedecked, sometimes nude or semi-nude. In Beaton's photograph, the models function as fashionable *femmes fatales*, embodying, so to speak, the inevitable fate of modernist subversion: the relegation of high art to the subordinate role of mere backdrop for (shudder!) feminine fashion, with fashion itself functioning as the easy-to-grasp sign of the fleeting and the fickle, high art's deplorable Other. Cecil Beaton in his fashion photo, has indeed transformed Pollock's painting into "apocalyptic wallpaper," (to borrow Harold Rosenberg's term): perhaps not even apocalyptic — just pricey wallpaper.

But here, I must stop to deal with my own anger, my own rage. I must say that this comparison and its implications makes me angry — and uneasy — because it is hard to side with either of these visions of art or fashion. My anger, and my uneasiness, have to do with the fact that although I was involved in contemporary art in 1951, I was a young woman who was highly invested in fashion as well. And for me, in my early twenties (only a few years younger than Joan Mitchell), a struggling instructor, a graduate student and a faculty wife at Vassar, being fashionable was one of the things that helped me and my struggling contemporaries to constitute our difference from the women around us in the early fifties. Being elegant, caring about clothes constituted a form of opposition to what I called "little brown wrenism," a disease imported from Harvard by Vassar faculty wives and their spouses along with the post-war revival of "kinder kirche kuche." It was premised on a "womanly," wifely, properly subordinate look: no makeup, shapeless tweeds, dun coloured twin sets, sensible shoes, ferocious domesticity, like helping hubby type his dissertation or even supercrap like weaving your children's pinafores or sewing your husband's shirts. Brilliance, brain, ambition *had* to be marked as different. There were several possibilities: for artists like Joan Mitchell or for Grace Hartigan, paint-stained jeans and a black turtleneck could be professional attire and constitute an assertion of difference at the same time. A strong-minded British eccentric like the philosopher, Elizabeth Anscombe insisted on complete menswear: jacket, tie, trousers and shirt. I am told that a special podium which hid the offending pants had to be rigged up when she lectured at Barnard College. As a woman who followed fashion, I could have told you who the model was in the Cecil Beaton photograph, just as easily as I could identify Jackson Pollock. And I could have told you who had designed the splendid gown she wore. My grandmother had given me a subscription to *Vogue* when I was still in high school and I followed fashion, as I followed art, avidly. I certainly knew they were not the same thing, but my passionate involvement with both art and fashion (and I might add, anti-MacCarthy politics) at the time made the fact that I was a woman, not a man, and a woman who thought of herself as different from many of the women around her, a vital differential in my relation to the elements of the Beaton versus Namath opposition.

What then, are we to make of a picture of Joan Mitchell at work in front of her painting, *Bridge*, taken by Rudy Burckhardt in 1957? (See Bernstock, 1988:212, top for reproduction) Where should it be placed? In the camp of the original, authentic creator, like the Pollock photograph, or in that of the Beaton model? She is, after all, like the model, an attractive, slender young woman. I don't know whether Joan Mitchell ever saw the *Vogue* photo, and she was certainly not interested in fashion, but the oppositions offered by the two images were certainly part of the context within which she lived and worked.

Different though they may be as visual objects, the position of the model in the *Vogue* picture is not so different from that of Willem de Kooning's *Woman* at the time. Both Beaton's photograph and De Kooning's painting implied that woman's place was as object of the image rather than creator of it. Her rage was to be not the "rage to paint" but rather, to be "all the rage." The Burckhardt photo of Mitchell, then, is something of an anomaly, the object taking over the subject position, albeit with a difference. And this, despite the fact that Mitchell's body, qua body, is an athletic, dynamic, active one — as active in the picture-making process as Pollock's. Mitchell herself had been a successful ice-skater and always moved with assertive energy and economy. Yet in terms of the Namath and the Beaton photos, she is twice "othered": once as the female "other" of the male Jackson Pollock, but once again as the female "other" of the elegant and proper female *Vogue* fashion model.

In other photos taken in front of her work, Mitchell is made to seem less self-assured, less "one of the boys." But there is one photograph taken in about 1953, of Joan Mitchell and her poodle, George, that brings to mind one of the most famous youthful self-images of the artist as a young subversive, Courbet's *Self Portrait with a Black Dog* of 1842. In the photograph of Mitchell and her dog, although she is clearly the "other" of Courbet in terms of gender, Mitchell may now be seen as "same" in terms of the chosen elements of the artist's self-representation: like Courbet, possessing her work and her dog on the model of male self-imagery. Mitchell's otherness, in the photograph, swerves back, in this trajectory, to identity; her rage is transformed into mastery, envisioned as a positive vector in the process of creation. For a photographic instant, at least, "as if" is seen as reality, Mitchell is one of the boys — Courbet, a very big boy indeed. And yet, this is not a completely satisfying resolution to the dilemma of the woman artist. We do not see the brush in Mitchell's hand, after all, as we do in Courbet's in the centre of his *Studio* and we all know, from simplified Freud if not from various artists and art critics, that the brush is the phallic symbol par excellence. Artists have even been said to paint with their pricks — and how can a woman do that? As Michael Leja has succinctly put it: "A dame with an Abstract Expressionist brush is no less a misfit than a *noir* heroine with a rod." (Leja, 1993: 262)

What a wholesome emotion rage is—or can be! "Menin aida thea Peleadeo Achileus.... Sing goddess the wrath of Achilles..." The *Iliad* starts on the high note of rage, connecting art itself — the singing of the goddess — with heroic anger. Nietszche extolled the salutary potential of rage, above all, when it engaged the creative psyche. So did William Blake, who declared "The tigers of wrath are wiser than the horses of instruction." Yet how unbecoming rage and the energy generated by it, is thought to be when it comes from a real woman. And all too often, women's rage is internalized, turning the justifiable fury they feel both against the social institutions and the individuals that condemn them to inferior status not on others, but on *themselves*: cutting up their own work; making it small; rejecting violence and force as possessions of the masculine ego, hence unavailable to the female artist; stopping work altogether; speaking in a whisper instead of a shriek; becoming the male artist's support system. Silence has always been a viable, indeed, a golden, alternative for women artists. The fact that Mitchell, though a woman, could take possession of her rage and, like a man, make it into a rage to paint: this was a more difficult concept for a male dominated art world to accept.

Yet it would seem to me that rage, and its corollary, rage to paint, are both central to the project of Joan Mitchell. Mitchell herself quite overtly rejected the notion of femininity attached to her work, although she came to accept the notion of feminism as a political stance. Her paintings forcefully help establish the notion of a feminine Other — energetic, angry, excessive, spilling over the boundaries of the formless, the victimized, the gentle or the passive — but battling, at the same time those other familiar demons, those of chaos and hysteria, with a kind of risky *ad hoc* structure.

In a long, rambling, beautifully revealing letter she wrote to me probably in the late 80s, Joan says "... I have lots of real reasons to hate ... and somehow I can't ever get to hatred unless someone is kicking my dog Marion (true story) ... or destroying Gisèle (a friend) etc., and then I'll bite — (I can't get to killing — my "dead" shrink kept trying to get me there — I have never made it — my I loved her.)" (Joan Mitchell, letter to the author, undated) Perhaps she never thought of herself as angry, in rage: I don't suppose she thought of herself as a heavy drinker, an alcoholic, either, Neither did the various male artists who depended on rage and alcohol either to stimulate their art or at least, to make it possible for them to write or paint and not succumb to darkness and passivity.

Recently, however, women have been discovering the specificity of their rage and anger and writing about it. In 1993, in an article entitled "Rage Begins at Home," literary scholar Mary Ann Caws begins by differentiating rage from anger, asserting: "Rage is general, as I see it, and is in that quite unlike anger — specific or motivated by something — which can, upon occasion, be calmed by some specific solution, beyond what one can state or feel or see. Rage is, I have come to think, one of the great marvels of the universe, for it is large, lithe, and lasting. I have come to treasure my rage, as I never could my anger.... My rage possessed and is still undoubtedly possessing me, from inside, and did not, does not, cannot demand that I control it. ...Energy comes from, and is sometimes indistinguishable from this rage I mean...." But later Caws ceases to differentiate between the two, for, as she puts it, "I believe they have me both." (Caws, 1993:65–66) In 1992, in a special issue of *RE search* entitled "Angry Women," in an interview with Avital Ronell, Andrea Juno declares: "The only way a woman can escape an abusive misogynistic relationship is through full-fledged anger. Anger may also be the conduit by which women in general can free themselves from larger social oppressions." Avital Ronell replies: "Anger must not be confined to being a mere *off-shoot* or ressentimental, festering wounds, but must be a channeling or broadcast system that, through creative expression, produces a certain *community*. That image of a mythical, Medusan threat is wonderful..." (Ronell and Juno, 1992:151) For Mitchell, rage, or anger, was singular, consuming — no sense of community or connection could be constructed through it between herself and other women. Nevertheless, I think we must be aware of the power of individual anger in women's achievement, as revealed in the work of Mitchell and many others of her generation — and after.

Yet without Joan Mitchell's unerring sense of formal rectitude, without her daring and her discipline as a maker of marks and images, her work would be without interest. I would like to look now at a series of images that have often escaped careful examination: the series of ten original multi-coloured lithographs, drawn on aluminum plates, that the artist made in 1981 with Master Printer Kenneth Tyler. These works are in some ways anomalous in the artist's oeuvre in that they are both small scale and are *not* executed in oil paint, Mitchell's preferred medium. And yet for that very reason, because they are, let us say, more approachable, they offer a good starting place to chart the intersection of energy and its articulation in Mitchell's work — the explicit way meaning comes into being in her imagery. Delicacy grace and awkwardness are all present in varying degrees in Mitchell's subtle, non-referential calligraphy. Same and different constantly play their role in the production of these prints' meaning, which, though visual in every respect nevertheless shares in the distinctive character of language itself in constructing its objects.

How do visual structures of similarity and difference come into play in a reading of two of these Bedford lithographs, *Bedford I* and *Bedford III*? In both lithographs, a bottom layer, which we see as earth or ground, is opposed to an airier, more lightly applied blue "sky" area above. Yet the feeling, or the mood of each of these prints is very different, the vernal lightness, sprouting bounce and dancing rhythms of *Bedford I* creates an utterly opposing atmosphere to that of petulant, indeed, outright angry animation, created by the black, more solid facture of the choppy ground element and the fractured sky area of *Bedford III*. In yet another print from the same series, *Flower III*, a four-colour lithograph, the relationship between more densely worked and more open areas is reversed: now it is the upper portion of the image that is more filled with colour and incident and meshed strokes of crayon, while the bottom of the piece is more sketchily adumbrated by a series of open vertical strokes which leave plenty of leeway for the white paper beneath.

Two polarities of Joan Mitchell's style are demonstrated in a later group of prints she created in conjunction with Tyler Graphics. In *Sunflowers II* of 1992, two related images are juxtaposed to form a diptych: the subject is really the relation of the downpouring energy of the crayon strokes: these dark, congested rectangles have nothing in common with Van Gogh's famous flowers except the palpitating excitement of their facture. But there is something perverse about the title: these are dark sunflowers indeed, the one on the right, with its thick, blotchy smears of blue and green pigment and skinny bent supports is especially ominous. In *Little Weeds II*, of the same date, however, the colours are brighter, the calligraphy dispersed over a broader, emptier horizontal field, the mood more frenetic, the dynamic centrifugal rather than contained.

From the very beginning, Mitchell's rage to paint was marked by a very specific battle between containment and chaos. In *Red Painting No. 2* of 1954, a shivering island of agitation is held in check by its central focus, the mazing and amazing dynamism of the brushwork pulled together and layered in deep, jewel-coloured skeins. A close-up detail of the upper central portion of the canvas reveals something of the complexity of Mitchell's facture, the almost excessive bravado of the gestural centre compared to the cool pallor of the gridded margins, as though something wild had escaped from a cage — or needed to be pent up in one.

Mitchell's work has often been compared to that of her contemporaries and immediate predecessors. It is certainly interesting to compare Mitchell's *Untitled* of 1956-57 with De Kooning's *Woman* of 1949-50. (University of North Carolina, Greensboro, Weatherspoon Art Gallery) We compare the work of abstract artists to other works of art, both abstract and representational because that in essence is all that there is to compare them to. Abstract art works in a context of painting and its strategies: there is no external "object" to compare with the art-work to see if the artist "got it right." Comparing Mitchell's painting with De Kooning's, we see that she accepted the sweep, the slash, the bravura brushwork of his style, but rejected what is most striking about his image: the figuration. Comparison, of course, can bring out difference as well as similarity. Much is sometimes made of the "impact" or "influence" of Mitchell's long time companion, the Canadian-born abstractionist, Riopelle, on her style. Yet I think comparison in this case brings out irrevocable difference: Riopelle's patterning is more regular, less aleatory, more all-over, of equal density throughout, which gives his work a preconceived rhythmic formula utterly opposed to Mitchell's poignant visual searching.

In Mitchell's work, as I am trying to demonstrate, meaning and emotional intensity are produced structurally, as it were, by a whole series of oppositions: oppositions of dense versus transparent strokes; gridded structure versus more chaotic, ad hoc construction; weight on the bottom of the canvas versus weight at the top, light versus dark; choppy versus continuous brush strokes; harmonious and clashing juxtapositions of hue — all are potent signs of meaning and feeling.

It is this structural freedom and control, this complexity of vision that accounts for the fact that, far from being a one-note painter, Mitchell's work exhibits a vast *range* of possibilities, from the spreading, ecstatic panoramas to the inward curdling "black paintings," from the totally covered canvas to the canvas enlivened only with a few dashes of calligraphy. *Field for Two* of 1973 (Collection Joanne and Philip Von Blon, Minneapolis, Minnesota) could almost be a Rothko, but a Rothko highly implicated in Hans Hoffman's "push and pull." The gridded planes of colour hover over and retreat from the surface of the canvas: And what colours they are! Pinks, oranges, a touch of vernal green — and then those streaks of hovering darkness which so often seem designed to disrupt easy comfort or harmony in Mitchell's best canvases.

The diptych — a two-canvas format, the triptych — a three-canvas format, and the polyptych — a multiple-canvas format — attracted Mitchell increasingly from the late sixties on. Of course, the two part or multipartite format was not Mitchell's invention. On the contrary, it had had a long history, going back to the religious art of the Middle Ages and Renaissance, when it often assumed heroic proportions in the traditional Christian altarpiece. More recently, in the fifties, Jackson Pollock had made use of both the diptych and the polyptch in a series of dramatic drip paintings where strings of pigment jumped over barriers and responded to similar formations in their partner paintings.

But Mitchell's multi-canvas creations were different from both the religious art of the past and Pollock's more recent essays in the genre as well. First, they constituted a response to her own need for greater spatial expansiveness, yet an expansiveness that would nevertheless be held in check by the specific dimensions of the individual panels that constituted the multiple-object. Secondly, the diptych or polyptych appealed to her because of the greater complexity of relationships it could induce: not just the play of difference and analogy *within* the single canvas, but response and reaction against another, related panel, both like and different. The range of these interrelated expressions was vast and open-ended. At times, the notion of landscape, and the topographic almost inevitably enters the mind of the spectator. There are titles, like *Plowed Field*, *Weeds*, *The Lake*, or *River* which conjure up a topographic or landscape experience. The fact that Mitchell lived for a great deal of her mature life in Vétheuil, on the Seine, with its splendid views already immortalized by Monet (who had lived briefly in the gardeners' cottage of her property) increases the temptation to ascribe specific paintings to precise locales, actual landscape inspiration. But it is important to keep in mind that almost all of Mitchell's canvases were titled *after* the fact, not before. Far from being a painter who worked "sur le motif," like Monet or Cézanne, one might say that Mitchell was a painter who worked the motif in after: she discovered the analogies to some thing, place or idea or feeling *after* she had completed the work, not before. Many of the titles are facetious or arcane, like *The Goodbye Door* or *Salut Tom*. Some of them are flatly descriptive like *Cobalt* or *Bottom Yellow*. But in all of them, we are aware of what art critic Barbara Rose denominated the "struggle between coherence and wild rebellion." (Rose, 1981:5) That, if anything, is what Mitchell's paintings are "about." As such, they constitute a pictorial palimpsest of multiple experiences; they are never, perfect, finished objects. From their brazen refusal of harmonious resolution rises their blazing glory.

In a wonderfully suggestive article about Virginia Woolf and Duke Ellington which appeared in the *New York Times* on 1 November 1999, cultural critic Margo Jefferson turned her thoughts to "the place of beauty and fury in Woolf's work." And she goes on to say "Beauty restores and fury demolishes in her novels. The bond between them ... is so psychically fraught it remains muted, even subterranean." But, Jefferson continues, "Like grief or longing or moments of transcendence. ...anger can be changed into something else and made new." She ends her piece by asserting that "elegy and fury [may exist] side by side, beauty and the heart of darkness sharing one language."

How apt a description this is of Joan Mitchell's painting at its best, an art in which rage and the rage to paint so often coincide, and indeed, share the same, ever questing, always un-formulaic pictorial language.

My next allegorical example will be Jenny Saville, and the concept of

Truth. But before we turn to the concept of truth, or rather a problematization of that concept, in the nudes of Jenny Saville, we need to refresh our memories with some images of nudes of the recent past, for these classical nineteenth century examples by the French academician Bouguereau and the ex-vanguardist-Impressionist, Renoir. Nothing could be further from the truth of the female body, than these classicizing, naturalizing confections, designed it would seem to satisfy the visual appetites of the French *homme moyen sensuel*, without giving him a heart attack or an erection. Flesh is smoothed over, irregularities are tactfully concealed, classical precedent and tradition varnish over the immediacy of visceral response to the naked female form and transform it into High Art.

Territories was the name of Saville's recent show at the Gagosian Galleries and the title is an apt one. The mapping of fleshly geography rather than the fatness of individual form seems an appropriate nomenclature for these figures which however superficially Rubensian (one is actually entitled *Ruben's Flap*), however much a slap in the face of today's waif-obsessed female culture they may be at times — are other things as well. The immediate visual impact is one of excess. These are huge paintings. *Ruben's Flap* is almost 350 cm by 244 cm. Gargantuan naked bodies hurtle away from us back into space or implode into our space — seductive, yet somehow injured flesh extrudes onto the picture plane with an uncanny combination of delicate brushwork and brutal slathering of pigment in a perspectival extravagance that at once bespeaks the objectivity of the photograph and the empathetic angst of Expressionism. But Saville's achievement goes beyond mere excess, into more interesting truth-related territory.

First of all the subjects of *Territories* can hardly be categorized as women without some difficulty. Rather they float in that indefinable postmodern realm of gender nirvana brilliantly theorized by Judith Butler, a realm of shifting identities, loosened gender categories, and rejection of essential difference between female and male. Truth one might say to the shifty nature of human sexuality. In its aggressive anti-essentialism, Saville's work is much an intellectual project, a social construction of the body, as it is neo-Rubensian or one up on Lucien Freud. Even the brushwork, juicy as it is, is, in a sense intellectualized — immensely self-conscious and self-revealing as it goes about its business of welding male to female, making a visual rhyme between problematic genitalia and lusciously rose-slathered, daringly foreshortened thigh, in the truly ambiguous and hugely disturbing *Matrix I* (1999).

Did I say that these works were upsetting? Because they are, as truth telling, especially truth in the realm of the sexual generally is. It is one thing to talk about the arbitrariness of gender categories; it's another to demonstrate it in pigment on canvas. What makes these images even more disturbing is the formal language, which inscribes a similar ambiguity, even ambivalence, between the assertive pictorial naturalism of the bodily subject matter and the openly painterly substance of the signifiers. It is this disjunction between form and content, as well as the uncanny re-figuration of sexuality itself, that allies Saville the painter with other women artists working in the field of gender shock — Cindy Sherman for instance, in her photographed sex dolls, or the sculptor Kiki Smith.

This is not the "return to painting" so fervently desired by conservatives and derided by radicals. One might say literally that Saville's work is post post-painterly, to wrench this term out of its original context: painterliness pushed so far over the top that it signifies a kind of disease of the pictorial, a symptom of some deep disturbance in the relation of pigment to canvas. Although the surface and the grid both play an important role in Saville's formal language, both are melted down and sharpened up by the virtuoso brushwork that marks her style. Think Thomas Mann's *Dr. Faustus* and the whole idea current earlier in the century, or art as a kind of fatal spiritual disease.

Above all, this is a return to painting mediated by the photograph. Saville herself says that she dislikes painting from life and prefers photographic models. All of her monumental nudes are based on photographic precedents, but not in any simple way. She collects illustrations from pathology textbooks, photographs of bruises and injuries, family pictures, and most of her models are herself. But no one would consider them under the rubric of "self-portraiture" any more than one would think of a Cindy Sherman *Untitled* in such terms.

Matrix on the left involves a unambiguous crotch shot of a highly ambiguous nude body, in this case, not merely a photo-collaged construction, but an actual transsexual — De la Grace Volcano — whose mustache, tattoo, and clipped head assort oddly with his pouting breasts and — foregrounded — his richly impastoed vagina. The conjunction of bloody wound and masculine head brings to mind Freud's classical theory of castration, at the same time that it recalls Luce Irigaray's radically anti-phallocratic redefinition of female sexuality in terms of multiple sites of pleasure, endless *jouissance*. Yet *Matrix* can hardly be read as a pictorial sermon on a theme by Irigaray. We are constantly made aware that this is a painting about the very possibility of painting at the end of the century — the impossible possibility of telling the truth about the human body by means of oil on canvas at this particular moment of visual history. The exaggerated foreshortening, the slab-like rosy impasto on the thigh that almost seems to leap out of the canvas at us, but above all the securing of the surface by means of the gray horizontal plane beneath the body and the elegant tattoo on the vertical arm that intersects with it — all of these strategies recall both the traditions of modernism and the anxieties of post modern representation, with all its implications for a frighteningly truthful neo-realism. Even the least "bodily" of the images is disturbing, the canvas called *Hyphen* (1999) which represents Jenny herself on the right with her sister, an image evidently taken from a childhood photo — an enormous painting. I am not sure why this is the case, but this seemed to be the most shockingly sexual of all the images on view, perhaps because in the absence of the naked body, all the voluptuous indulgence of the flesh is displaced onto the heads alone and concentrated there, as though the pouting too-red lips are analogues for sex organs, the childishly rounded cheeks, buttocks.

I will take the work of Rachel Whiteread, a British sculptor and installation artist (born in London in 1963, and recipient of the prestigious Turner prize in 1993), as an allegory of Justice.

Whiteread made her first impression on the public — and it was a noisy and contested one — with her ephemeral suces de scandal *House*, which existed from October to December of 1993 on an undistinguished site in London's East End. In basing her monument on the technique of casting — here, casting the interior of an abandoned house in concrete — Whiteread resorts to a time-honoured sculptural practice. What is novel and startling is the way she reconfigures the casting mode, for in the process of recording the appearance of an ordinary house, the inside becomes the outside; what was hidden from view receives its due in the light of day in the most absorbing and complete detail. In short, justice is done to ordinary spaces and surfaces, but only at the price of destroying space and surface — putting the object to death to save it so to speak. In its uncanny unhiddenness, *House* created an immense public furore, ranging from high-culture defenders of it as "art" to popular dismissal of it as trash or an eyesore or a publicity stunt; reactions ranged from those who saw it as an appeal for more public housing to those who considered it a sharp criticism of the Thatcher government and its cutbacks. *House* was news during its brief existence, arousing responses in the form of graffiti inscribed on its surface and clever articles by leading theoreticians of contemporary art. And one might say that justice was done to its importance as a site of dialogue and conflict even in the very fact of its untimely destruction. To go still further in our allegorization of *House*, some might say, as did art-historian Jon Bird, that *House* signified a "metaphorical inversion of the body, a reversal of interiority and exteriority that rendered the private public and made the public a site for democratic exchange." (Bird, 1994:122)

This is particularly true of a work that served as preparation for *House*, *Ghost* of 1990, the cast of an entire room of a derelict house in north London. Inevitably, people think of work like this, transferred to the gallery setting, as a kind of shrine or memorial, an object transcending its humble origins by reason of its aesthetic or moral value. Yet this is precisely what works like these refuse or reject. The original object, in all its gritty and commonplace uniqueness remains, asserts itself, however ambiguously. Is the original room on which *Ghost* is based present or absent in the work itself?

The casting process itself, as Jon Bird points out, repeats the play of presence and absence. Traditionally the mould is discarded and the cast is left as the "supplement" to the original. Whiteread utilizes this familiar technique but introduces an alarming twist, for what is the cast supplementary to? The original is a space, a nothingness or void. Crudely put, one may say that Whiteread's work does justice, not merely to the humble objects of everyday experience, but paradoxically, to nothingness itself, giving concrete articulation to the void, solidifying emptiness.

Which is not to say that Whiteread is not devoted to doing justice to the specificity of the humble, fragmentary objects of our modern urban existence itself — the discards, the broken, the maimed and the rejected. In her series of R-type colour photographs of the late 1990s, works like *Bin: Coney Island* (1998–99) or *Furniture* (1994–98), she focuses on such minimalia as the garbage can or the discarded bathtub, and its accompanying detritus, conferring on them objectively and without sentimentality, a unique dignity, a restrained and objectified pathos. Who, looking at such images of displacement, is not reminded of the ultimate injustice of homelessness and the plight of the homeless in our prosperous urban centers?

Yet it is not through trivial analogy that Whiteread's objects produce their powerful if low-keyed effect; on the contrary it is by maintaining the specific contingencies, the concrete individuality, the bumps and blemishes of the cast subject itself that her work is made memorable and may stand as an allegory of the virtue of Justice. Unlike so much contemporary work, Whiteread's casts reject either seriality or multiplicity in favor of a poignant uniqueness. Indeed, as Rosalind Krauss has pointed out: "Whiteread's work self-evidently attaches itself ... to the whole array of indexically produced forms that extends from death masks to photographs, all of these resonant with the sense that they have been cast (whether physically or optically) from 'life'." "And," she continues, "like the death mask and the photograph ... this work is continually moving through a funerary terrain, a necropolis of abandoned mattresses, mortuary slabs, hospital accoutrements ... condemned houses." (Krauss, 1996–97: 76, 80) Krauss sees Whiteread's practice as a sort of resistance to exchange value or metaphor, a resistance which can also be thought of, in allegorical terms, as a kind of justice, however, rough, accorded to the intractable quiddity of the thing.

An even more startling and original engagement with justice is constituted by Whiteread's casts of, not objects, no matter however humble, but the spaces beneath or between them: In the case of *Untitled (100 Spaces),* cast in resin in 1996, it is the spaces beneath chairs that are in question, patiently cast in translucid, jewel-toned resin. Now this seems to me justice on a high scale to make casts of the underneaths of chairs. Certainly, it is one of our most neglected experiences of daily life, but underneath the chair is a vital experience as anyone who has tried to get her feet under the space beneath her seat and finds it occupied. The social inevitably inserts itself into our experience of these resins, conveying a sense of the ungainly uniqueness of each individual seat in its gallery imposed row, suggesting the uncanniness of the banal itself when it presents itself to the viewer in such an unexpected form.

Recently, Whiteread has taken on the task of creating public monuments, whether they be as unnoticeable as her New York *Soho Watertower*, which alternately blends into the urban fabric with near invisibility, or, under other circumstances, hoves into view like a beatific visitation from another planet. And ultimately of course justice can no better be allegorized than in her Vienna Judenplatz Holocaust memorial. This memorial is constituted by the cast of the interior of a library "to be placed in the centre of a square of modest dimensions." The casting of the library was done from its interior so that instead of the spines of the books being visible, the invisible, more idiosyncratic portions of them, the pages and the spaces between the books, and the backs of the shelves are projected on the exterior surface. One might perhaps remember in contemplating this memorial, that the Jews have always identified themselves as the "People of the Book" and more darkly, one might think back to the dreadful desecration wrought by Nazi book-burning and its premonition of still darker and more horrifying burnings to follow: the destruction of the Jews of Europe in the furnaces of Auschwitz. By confronting us with the hidden interiors of these books in a situation that commemorates one of the major outrages of our time, Whiteread, without resorting to naturalistic sentimentality makes the unspeakable available for contemplation. In this case, Whiteread's work no longer needs to be read as an allegory of justice. It assumes the painful task of doing the work of justice itself.

I hope this allegorical examination of the work of three women artists has not taken you too far a field from the topic of this conference: *Culture and Humanity in the New Millennium: The Future of Human Values.* Or maybe I hope that it has, and that in its sheer specificity its lack of more general claims of universal meaning or global profundity, this work may point to the future — the immediate future that is, of both visual art, art-criticism and art-history. As for the future of human values per se, I can do no better than to refer to the *New York Times* (Op-Ed) piece I referred to earlier and declare with Joyce Carol Oates, "Though I lack a vision of the twenty-first century, I have been granted a vision of the idyllic thirty-first century, where all the men are beautiful, all the women are strong, and all the children are clones of media celebrities and favourite pets. But no one has yet asked me about the thirty-first century."

Notes

1. 1964 Exhibition Catalogue, New York, Robert Miller Gallery, 1994, np. See no. for illustration.
2. See T. J. Clark, *Farewell to an Idea*, New Haven, 1999 and Serge Guilbault, *Reconstructing Modernism*, Cambridge, Mass, 1991, passim. for this notion. The Beaton photo appears on the cover of Guilbaut's book.

References

Bernstock, Judith (1988). *Joan Mitchell*, New York: Hudson Hills Press.

Bird, Jon (1994). *House*, p. 122.

Caws, Mary Ann (1993). "Rage Begins at Home." *Massachusetts Review*, pp. 65–66.

Day, Gail (1999). "Allegory: Between Deconstruction and Dialectics." *Oxford Art*, Vol. 22, No. 1, pp. 103–18.

De Kooning, Elaine, and Rosalyn Drexler (1973). "Dialogue." Thomas Hess and Elizabeth Baker, eds., *Art and Sexual Politics*. New York: Collier, pp. 56.

Krauss, Rosalind (1996–97). "X Marks the Spot." F. Bradley, ed., *Rachel Whiteread: Shedding Life* (Exhibition Catalogue). Tate Liverpool, pp. 76, 80.

Leja, Michael (1993). *Reframing Abstract Expressionism: Subjectivity and Painting in the 1940s*. New Haven, p. 262.

Ronell, Avital, and Andrea Juno (1992). "Angry Women." *RE search*, p. 51.

Rose, Barbara (1981). *Joan Mitchell: Bedford Series: A Group of Ten Color Lithographs*. Bedford, New York, p. 5.

Confucianism in the Twenty-first Century: Dialogue Among Civilization and the Public Intellectual

Tu Wei-ming

I am privileged to have this rare opportunity to share a few of my still evolving thoughts on Confucianism humanism. The story of Confucian and humanism — trans-temporal, cross-cultural and cross-disciplinary — is too long, too complicated, and to some maybe too frustrating and for me, too personal, to be told except for some synoptic and necessarily subjective notes. I would like to begin with maybe a glimpse of what I consider the basic spiritual orientation of Confucian humanism and whether they help orient our thoughts to that particular domain. I would like to share with you two quotes from the Confucian classics: one, a very short passage from the centrality or commonality of *Doctrine of the Mean* to give you a sense of the highest ideal of human flourishing in the Confucian context.

> Only those who are most sincere can fully realize their own nature. Able to fully realize their own nature they can fully realize their nature of humanity. Able to fully realize the nature of humanity, they can fully realize the nature of things. Able to fully realize the nature of things, they can take part in the transforming and nourishing process of heaven and earth. Able to take part in the transforming and nourishing process of heaven and earth, they can form a trinity with heaven and earth.

The highest Confucian idea of human self-realization then, is the unity between human and heaven.

The other statement is a bit mundane but it is one of the most critical points from the *Great Learning*. For the ancients

> who wished to illuminate their illuminating virtue throughout the world, they must first govern their states. To govern their states they must harmonize their families, wishing to harmonize their families, they must cultivate their bodies, wishing to cultivate their bodies, they must rectify their hearts and minds. Wishing to rectify their hearts and minds, they must purify their intentions. Wishing to purify their intentions, they must extend their knowledge. The

extension of knowledge lay in the study of things. Only when things are studied is knowledge extended. Only when knowledge is extended can intentions be purified. Only when intentions are purified, can minds and hearts can be rectified. Only when minds and hearts are rectified, can bodies be cultivated. Only when bodies are cultivated, can families be harmonized. Only when families are harmonized, can states be governed. Only when states are governed, can there be peace throughout the world.

Now, based on these two rather short statements, we can through some kind of imagination construct the basic agenda of Confucian humanism. The kind of humanism that ought to be inclusive, integrated, and comprehensive, in sharp contrast with the humanism that emerged in the modern West. I will have to address that issue later. You may want to conceive the Confucian project as a series of concentric circles, extending from the person, including the interiority of the person as well as the person of the body, heart and mind as soul and spirit and extending gradually to an ever-expanding network of relations. You have to imagine that the outer realm of that extension is always open—it is not even anthropocentric, we have to go beyond anthropocentrism to fully understand the meaning of Confucian humanism.

We may also want to specify that there are four inseparable dimensions through this comprehensive humanism. One is the question of the self, not self as the body or heart and mind, but self as soul and spirit. The second dimension is community variously understood as the nuclear family as a clan, as a village, society, nation, as the global community, and people even say that we should go beyond the global family to the family of the cosmos — you have to imagine community variously defined. The third dimension is nature and the fourth one, I will simply characterize as the way of heaven.

There are four principles governing these four dimensions. Integration of the self — the first question of Confucian philosophy is self-cultivation, is very much in line with the Greek idea of "know thyself" and requires continuous interaction between body and mind and soul and spirit. So an integrated person is considered as an accomplished person. The second one is a fruitful interaction between self and community but also between community and community. The third one is a sustainable and harmonious relationship between human species as a whole and nature. Nature is not the full story, for heaven cannot simply be reduced to nature as some scholars in China have insisted that heaven is an expression of nature. But I insist that heaven is something that overflows beyond the natural world which therefore gives rise to the idea of mutuality or mutual responsiveness between the human heart and mind and the way of heaven.

These four dimensions put together, with the series of concentric circles, give us a glimpse of the Confucian humanistic project or humanistic agenda. Of course we are not just talking of the ideal of human flourishing, we are also talking about power and influence, since after all we are talking of the tradition that has been powerful in East Asia for centuries, China, Vietnam, Korea and Japan. Before the turn of the century, every educated person was exposed to this form of learning. Therefore family ethics, political culture, social organization and all forms of human interrelatedness, world view, what we would call life orientation, was very much shaped by this comprehensive, integrated, inclusive humanism. Yet of course the story has to begin with not a glorification of this humanistic tradition, but how it was marginalized and actively rejected by some of the most brilliant minds in East Asia in the last one hundred years or so.

There is no need for me to underscore the importance of the dominant ethos in the modern world — what I called the "enlightened" mentality, either in its capitalistic or socialistic orientations. A portion of the enlightenment mentality that emerged in the West in the seventeenth century continued to be very powerful as spheres of interest such as the market economy, democratic polity, civil society, not to mention science and technology. Even our concept of universities is very much a part of this particular ethos, is also a form of humanism. You could say that humanism of the modern West has thoroughly deconstructed the humanism, no matter how beautiful it is constructed, in my description of Confucianism. But this process that we characterize as Westernization, or modernization, or recently as globalization, involves science and technology, information flow, finance, capital, trade, migration and of course pollution and disease. It is such a powerful process of transformation that the Confucian humanistic world order has been deconstructed and underlying this powerful process of modernization are some basic and universalizable and fully universalized values such as liberty, rationality, due process of law, human rights and dignity of the person.

This marginalized Confucianism appears to be very different from what I described in a highly idealized sense. In the minds of some of the most articulate, brilliant intellectuals in modern China, this agriculture-based economy, family-centred society, paternalistic polity, the Confucian ideology for that kind of society was conservative, very hierarchical, authoritarian, male chauvinistic, and is not compatible with the industrial modern civilization, egalitarianism, freedom, not to mention science and democracy. So Confucianism has been marginalized as the feudal past, even in an innocuous way it could be museumized as a relic of the past and can also be conceived as ghosts, that it will have to be slain again and again so that China can become fully modernized.

In the context of the transformation of modern China, say the last three generations, more than one hundred years, one of the most or perhaps one of the longest continuous civilizations as many Chinese textbooks have shown us, also has a very short, and complicated modern memory. The ruptures of modern China have been so pronounced that you could say that, roughly from the Opium War (1839) to the founding of the People's Republic of China (1949), in every decade of that period there was a major restructuring of society. During the Taiping Rebellion, twenty million people were displaced — the combination of foreign powers, the failure of the Hundred-day Reform, the Boxer Rebellion, the 1911 Revolution, the international warfare of the world war period, Japanese aggression, and then of course the bloody conflict between the communists and the nationalists.

So every ten-year period roughly from 1839 to 1949 there was a major restructure of Chinese society. For people of our parents and grandparents generation, the possibility of three to four years of uninterrupted stable life was considered quite precious. Since 1949, every five years something dramatic happened. As soon as the People's Republic of China was established, there was the Korean War, the dramatic reconstructing continued with the Great Leap Forward of 1958, the three years of so-called great famine where probably more than thirty million people starved to death, and the Cultural Revolution which is now considered as the real holocaust of China. So China as being relatively stable only seems so since 1978-1979 with the reform and opening policy. Don't forget there was also Tiananmen.

The short memory and the collective, what we sometimes call the active and collective amnesia, characterizes the modern history of China. The story of Confucianism humanism has to be told against this background. I'll tell you one anecdote to give a sense of the situation. On the three-hundredth anniversary of the founding of Harvard University, more than six hundred guests were invited to represent six hundred universities. The prominent modern Chinese intellectual Hu Shi was invited as a representative of Peking University. According to Harvard ritual, guests were ranged according to the ages of their universities, so Hu Shi's position was 578 out of 600 guests. He said that he should have told them that Peking University is a continuation of the *tai xue,* of China, the imperial college, which would have been the oldest university, even older than the Egyptian university, but he was anti-Confucian and anti-tradition so he did not want to be associated with the feudal past. He wanted to be the new, and yet he was not particularly honoured.

I went as a representative of Harvard at the hundredth anniversary of Peking University in 1988. Peking University when it was established in the latter part of the nineteenth century, was radically different from the Peking University of May Fourth. The May Fourth Peking University was radically different from the Peking University of the republican period. After the founding of the People's Republic of China the whole place was moved to Yenjing University. Peking University before and after the Cultural Revolution was very, very different. So even over that one hundred years, I think that we are talking about four or five maybe six totally unconnected and disrupted periods.

Now, how can we even imagine in this context to talk about an outmoded, marginalized, deconstructed humanism no matter how beautiful it is so that we can reconstruct it in terms of classical texts and with a view to the twenty-first century. There are four very powerful trends that have emerged in the last thirty years or so, at the core of Western reflexivity that can provide a new context for this kind of discussion. Now when I say the last thirty years, I single out maybe 1968 as a very important turning point. In 1962 the American Academy of Arts and Sciences organized a special conference entitled "To the Year 2000" and the official publication from that conference was recently republished by MIT Press. People taking part at the conference were quite satisfied with their prophetic power. Daniel Bayer was at the conference, and I asked him if he had missed anything, he had said not much. "We missed two things, one is ecology, we had no idea that ecology or the environment would be so important, the other was we didn't know that the role of women would become so important." So they missed ecological consciousness and feminist sensitivity. I will say that these two, are two of the most powerful forces that have emerged in the modern West in the last thirty years. With ecology, the demand for going beyond anthropocentrism is so compelling, so powerful, that the mentality I have characterized as "enlightened" mentality is flawed in a very fundamental way, especially between humanity and nature.

In 1972, the first international conference on the environment was held in Stockholm. China sent a delegation and was the only group that refused to signed the preamble that was drafted by Maurice Strong, because there were two statements that the Chinese delegation did not like. One was the limit of growth and the other one was the limit of science and technology. The Chinese believe that there is no limit to growth and that every human problem can be solved by science and technology. That was 1972. Scientism still lingers on in China as of course does social engineering. But I think that right now, we must say that the faith in the transformative power of economic growth and science and technology has been problematized. I give you one example to show the importance of ecological sensitivity. I think that Dickenstein must have been the one who said that if you haven't died you never know the full meaning of life. If you have never been out of the earth, you never understand about the earth. None of us has died so none of us really fully understands the full meaning of life. But in the late 1960s we did manage as human beings to come out of the earth and look at it — and that sight became extremely good for understanding the last thirty years of this concerted effort to go beyond anthropocentricity.

A scholar in comparative religion made an observation, that if there is any prophet for the twentieth century, then it is the earth, because the earth is going to tell us what is permissible or not. Maybe the indigenous people are the teachers because they are using the term I just learnt at this conference, they managed to acquire the ability to listen deeply, "deep listening" to the voice of the earth. That was something beyond imagination thirty years ago.

Now we are familiar with feminism, and Professor Nochlin has just provided us with a marvelous example, a very evocative presentation of the power of the feminist perspective. In my point of view, I think one important implication for the rise of feminism as a form of humanism, is not simply the quest for gender equality, but a fundamental transformation of our conception of what is the family, what is a public place, for work, basic nature of human relationships, even the pattern of authority and power. Everything is being reconfigured, and even some of the basic values that I just pointed out, like liberty, rationality, due process of law, human rights, and the dignity of a person — these very values along with basic values and with the rights of a very feminist sensitivity, would have to augmented by some other powerful universalizable values such as justice and sympathy. Not just war, but civility and law; not just rights, but a sense of responsibility, not just the dignity of the person as an isolated individual, but the importance of understanding a person as the centre of relationships.

The third trend that is very important for my narrative is religious pluralism. Rudd Lubbers, who served as the prime minister of Holland for twelve years, told me in a joking way about his experience growing up in a Catholic community in Holland. He said that when he turned seventeen, he met his first Protestant, he liked the boy and was very surprised because he was a Protestant and not a Catholic. The possibility for anyone to experience that again is somewhat limited. There is a recent study of the religious landscape in the Boston area, and it is just amazing the kind of religions, especially new religions, represented there.

Even if Huntington is right in talking about the imminent "clash of civilizations" (and I have actually exchanged some ideas with him), then it is important for us to underscore the importance of dialogue with various civilizations, especially if we sense that the clash is imminent and become guardians of not just tolerance but coexistence of radically different religious orientations, mutual referencing through dialogue, a mutually beneficial way of understanding our religious situation or becoming part of the religious landscape or religious discourse. East Asia seems to have particular strength in multiculturalism or religious pluralism. In the 1960s, Ambassador Reischauer in his description of Japan says probably 70 percent of Japanese are Mahayana Buddhists, and 80 percent of them are also Shintoists. They are Buddhists and Shintoists, but they are also very much under the influence of Confucian ethics. So the possibilities of over-lapping of religious commitments, even the question of dual membership, of multiple memberships in religious communities have become rightly discussed.

The fourth trend would have to be global ethics. It is precisely because of religious pluralism, the diversity of the human situation, that there is a need to look for global ethics. But there are very different approaches. Hans Koon's approach is to find the minimum conditions for human coexistence, which is a kind of thinning process. If you look at his own biography he started with the communication between maybe two groups within the Catholic church, the Vatican, of which he was very critical, then the Catholics and the Protestants, then among three Abrahamic religions, Judaism, Christianity and Islam, and then seven so-called major historical religions including Buddhism, Hinduism, Moism, Confucianism, and most recently the communication between the religionists and the secularists. This was one approach. I think the United Nations, UNESCO, and a number of other projects including the Earth Charter, all tried to find some minimum conditions where human beings can coexist and eventually to mutually benefit in terms of their dialogue. In another approach, scholars like Marco Walksa and others, believe that even if we are successful in identifying some of the very basic principles that human beings will have to subscribe to we will still have to give and take. Now there are two principles, one in Chinese which is roughly translated as "do not do unto others what you do not want others do to you," which is the principle of reciprocity. It is probable more enforceable than the Christian idea of "do to others what you would like others do to you." But anyway it is a debatable issue.

The other one is the contingent principle of treating each person as an end, rather than simply a means to an end. But even if we can agree on a very faint description of a principle of human ethics it is important for the Christians, the Buddhists, the Hindus and Daoists to give a full account of human filiation from their perspective, for true dialogue and this idea to preach, to develop a kind of interaction between the minimum requirement and the maximum realization of one's idea of a person from a Christian, Buddhist or Hindu perspective, has created a lot of very interesting discussion in that general area of global ethics.

With the rise of ecological consciousness, feminist sensitivity, religious pluralism and global ethics, the question I want to pose is whether Confucian humanism, which has been marginalized and critiqued by some of the most brilliant minds in China, can still have some resources that can be retrieved, re-tapped and regenerated to help think through some of those issues. When I use that expression, I am really talking about issues from a pluralistic, multicultural point of view. I am not saying that this tradition has some exquisite claim and it can be considered as one of the many possible religious orientations for ethical, religious organizations. Now this is predicated on one observation, that globalizing process intensifies localization. All the primordial ties that are considered in our ordinary life situation, become more important for constructing our cultural identity today, partly because of globalization.

In fact, we can see the globalization of local conditions. Many religious movements are globalized, and it does not mean that they become cosmopolitan; it globalizes to highly local conditions. The interplay between global and local is such that we do not have an either/or choice. I do not think that it is possible to imagine a situation where we can emphasize the feeling that the World Economic Forum evokes talking about globalization as if the water tables would rise then every one would benefit, that kind of thing. That is very naive that the market economy has been very much criticized for. What are some of the primordial ties that we are talking about? — ethnicity, language, gender, land, class, age, faith. Since I have already written on some of these ideas, I am not going to elaborate on any of them.

For a while when I first went to the United States in the 1960s, the modernists really believed that modernization is a form of homogenization, one form of global transformation, and the developing societies attaching themselves to these primordial ties will have to give way to the more universalized modernizing process. But when I use the term primordial ties, I don't have this division between the third or the first world, in fact it is really global. If ethnicity as an issue is not properly dealt with as some in the United States have pointed out then the United States will become disunited. If language is not properly dealt with, like the official language issue in Canada and Belgium, there will be trouble. Gender is a universal issue as we know. As for questions of sovereignty, it is not simply a question of Palestinians or Taiwanese, but it is also Hawaiians, Native Americans, not to mention the Basques and numerous other groups in Europe.

We used to divide the world in terms of North and South. Now we have to divide the region, the country, the sub-region within a country, sometimes the same university between North and South. I am sure that people in the humanities are the South. We used to think about age in terms of thirty years, but now we have to think about age in age cohorts, in terms of ten years, or something like siblings, freshmen, seniors, as these groups have radically different concepts about rapid change. We used to worry about inter-religious conflict, we are now worried about more intra-religious conflict. Not just religious fundamentalism, Tibetan Buddhism, among others, cannot be totally free from this type of conflict. If we do not have a veto of choice, we need to learn to think beyond exclusive dichotomies, mind-body, spirit-matter, mental-physical, sacred-profane, to create-creature, East-West or even we-they.

We need to think in terms of complexity in our society in terms of quantifiable goods, such as economic capital, but also un-quantifiable, or at least extremely difficult to quantify other kinds of goods, that some people call social capital or communicative rationality. We need to think about competence not only in terms of scientific and technical competence we need to think about cultural competence. All the humanities are very much linked to the whole issue of human self-understanding and human self-reflexivity. That kind of cultural competence especially through generational transmission of values and ideas not to mention wisdom is that knowledge cannot be easily quantified. Cognitive intelligence can be quantified, but how about ethical intelligence, or emotional intelligence? Material conditions can be specified, but spiritual values are often very different.

Recently, I have been involved in a couple of projects, one is the question of traditions in modernity, not from traditions from the modern, but the continuous presence of traditions in modernity, in shaping different forms of modernity. The modernizing process has drastically restructured traditions, with the traditions themselves shaping the different forms of modernity. With multiple modernities we need to imagine, in fact we can show that the modernizing process may assume different cultural forms. One of the issues we need to talk about is the cultural implications of East Asian modernity. East Asia, at least in this part of East Asia, and certainly in Hong Kong is fully modernized, therefore it is Westernized, or some people would say Americanized. But the form or forms of life in East Asia are radically different. We have to account for that. I think that in the 1980s, scholars in Asia — Singapore, Malaysia and even in Hong Kong, were misled by the power of the Pacific region into thinking that the modernizing process, the dynamism of the modernizing process, had shifted from the Atlantic Ocean to the Pacific Ocean. With the financial crisis, that kind of confidence was somewhat dampened. However if we look at the emergence of East Asian modernity as a case in the past of the modernizing process it is not at all difficult for us to imagine the possibility in terms of the long haul, or for Southeast Asian modernity, South Asian modernity or Latin American modernity, Islamic modernity or African modernities. If we think in these terms from the one to the several, it is pluralism but not relativism.

We need to ask the question: What is the cultural message in the reemergence of China? Cultural China in particular? China not simply as an economic presence, a political power or a military power. Is there any cultural message or is it simply to take part in the global redistribution of goods defined in material terms or is there something deeper? It is in this connection that I would like to conclude with two observations concerning the reemergence of Confucianism, the possibility of some contributions that the Confucian tradition can make to this complicated modern, post-modern situation.

First of all, it is the core question of our inter-religious dialogue and multiple membership. The first Confucian-Christian dialogue was held right on this campus, a few years ago. I think Professor So and others took part in this discussion and I was very surprised when in the middle of the discussion I realized that of course I was quite aware of inter-religious dialogue, the Buddhists and the Christians, you knew who were the Buddhists and who were the Christians or the Muslims and the Jews. But in that Confucian-Christian dialogue, more than half the people represented the Confucian traditions were also Christians. They call themselves Catholic Confucians like De Bary and Julia Ching or Confucian-Protestants or Confucian-Methodists like John Bertrand and Bob Marrow. In 1995 I was invited to the University of Malaya for a Muslim-Confucian dialogue and a few scholars representing Muslims from China identified themselves as Confucian-Muslims. If you look at the situation in Taiwan, following the great tradition of Buddhism as a way of life of *tai xu*, then the humanistic Buddhism of *yin xun* and now *zhen yan* as Pure Land in this world *ren zhen jin tu*. All of them are involved in the discussion of Confucian ethics in such a way that they would not mind be classified as Confucian-Buddhists. So what does it mean when the word Confucian is used as an adjective in describing a particular form of Catholic, Protestant, Buddhist or Muslim? This leads on to the final point of the public intellectual.

I define a public intellectual in terms of a minimum requirement of three intra-connected ideas. Someone is characterized as a public intellectual if he or she is politically concerned, socially engaged and culturally sensitive or informed. Such a person on the surface comes out of an academic background, but in fact if you look at the situation in America, and in some European communities, only a small group of people in the academic community willingly assume the role of the public intellectual. The overwhelming majority of the people in the Academy just concern themselves with their own particular areas. But public intellectuals must function not only in the academic community but also in the mass media, in government, in business, in the professions, in religion and in all kinds of social movements. Especially the movements of ecology, human rights, consumer rights and so forth.

This modern conception of the public intellectual is something very rare in terms of human history. We are not talking about the modern representation of the ancient Greek idea of a philosopher, not the Judaic idea of a prophet, not the medieval idea of a priest, not the idea of a monk in a modern disguise, but something that fits very well with the tradition Confucian idea of the *shi*, a literatus, a scholar. When we ask the question, what is a Confucian Christian, a Confucian Christian is precisely someone who is politically concerned, socially engaged and culturally sensitive. If a Christian is only interested in the heaven yet to come, if the Buddhist is only interested in the other shore, in terms of one's own spiritual quest, then you cannot characterize such a Christian or such a Buddhist as a Confucian Christian or a Confucian Buddhist. So the word Confucian in this case gives a sense of political engagement, social concern and cultural sensitivity. Now this is possible for us to imagine especially if we look at the situation in mainland China and also broadly cultural China, which should not only include Taiwan, Hong Kong and Singapore, but also South Korea, Vietnam, Japan, overseas Chinese communities, and overseas East Asian communities.

We may have an interesting situation in the so-called Confucian world, a re-convergence of a kind of humanism, a kind of humanism which is not anthropocentric, the kind of humanism that is responsive to ecological concerns, to issues raised by feminists, to issues to religious pluralism and to a kind of global ethic that we are all very much interested in. The kind of humanism that would be able to formulate a critique very much in the spirit of the May Fourth intellectuals apart from the outmoded Confucian ideology that was agriculture-based, with an ideology that was family-centred, especially nepotism and male-chauvinism. So the trans-valuation of the Confucian values has already been done by three generations of scholars, first on the Mainland, then Hong Kong and outside and may provide an interesting case. I do not know how successful it would be as a form of knowledge that is very local, local in a very specific way. There are world religions that assume so many cultural forms that you cannot say that a particular cultural form is particularly characteristic of that religion. All three major world religions have that kind of characteristic. We cannot say that Buddhists in Thailand are more Buddhist than Buddhists anywhere else, or others are not as Islamic as Middle Eastern Muslims. But you have traditions that are so much tied to religious orientation that it is difficult to imagine that it is independent from that culture, for example, Shintoism in Japanese culture. Confucianism is somehow in-between. You cannot say that the Confucian tradition is not Chinese, or that the Confucian tradition is exclusively Chinese, because it is also Korean, Vietnamese and Japanese. It is in this particular context, that the issues raised may provide an example that a local form of knowledge may assume some global significance.

Roundtable Discussion

At the conclusion of the congress, a roundtable discussion was held with Professor S. T. Kwok as the Convenor. All the speakers at the Congress were invited to express their views on some of the themes that emerged over the course of the three days of talks. These themes include:

- Are there such things such as universal values?
- Can we accept pluralism over relativism as a guideline in developing a set of universal values?
- Can we find values to prioritize worth?
- Does globalization mean one outstanding value frame or can a plurality of representations sustain this process while maintaining critical values?
- What is the impact of the technological revolution on the humanities?
- How can music and literature remain significant in this scientific age?
- How will cultural revitalization will preserve and develop cultural legacies?

Professor Marc Ferro:

My question is connected with what Professor Tu Wei-ming has just discussed. He said that, in a way we feel that we are progressively becoming "foreigners in our country and in our own culture." I have already heard the sentence, "we are foreigners in our own country" on a number of occasions in this new century. First, from colonized countries, coming naturally from colonized people. Second, in south-western USA with Latinos, Chicanos who themselves feel that they are becoming foreigners in Arizona, California and so on. Third, in Russia, when the reforms of Peter the Great transformed the country, the south became poor, and St. Petersburg [Leningrad] became a foreign city for the great majority of Russians. Nowadays, as globalization begins to transform our political equilibrium, our democratic system, like France and other countries, the destruction of identity is coming from without, from foreigners. Of course, nationalism fights against this kind of thing. For Russia at the present time, the destruction is coming from without as well as within — and that is why it is hard for it to find a solution.

Professor Kato:

I would like to comment on whether there are any universal values. There are four things in France concerning technology, or more exactly the relentless advance of technology, which has had an influence on culture like literature, music and so on. I also mention the possible devaluation of a cultural tradition like Confucianism. I don't think that it is a very good strategy to try to pick out some universal values out of the list of all the values available, but if we attempt to fix up some virtues as universal and then they weaken, there is only the possibility for universal values — meta-values so to speak — the values that may work as a basis for discussion among the list of all the values. If you have some particular values, and encounter someone who negates them, then the whole discussion breaks down.

Foreigners are the precondition for civility of discussions between those who crave different values or different cultures — therefore foreigners act as kinds of meta-values, meta-cultures, vis-à-vis the pluralistic world of values and culture. Then, there is human life. Logically, it may be possible to argue that in the future, human life and the human world will be completely useless, that it is a dirty accident of the universe that it doesn't belong to humanity. But if you take this stand, then all our discussions then all our useless too, so we should yield to the previous speakers on the existence of universal values, the statement that human life has meaning. So it seems this sort of meta-value can be universal, but I think that a particular value linked to a historical culture cannot. The second point is technology. Mr. Wang Meng, argued the certain incompatibility between the technological world and literature and someone else has criticized this that the compatibility between technology and literature.

Now let us talk about literature, I am not at all underestimating the threatening influence of technology on literature. This is my second argument. It almost seems to me to be destiny, that the battle has already been lost for literature due to the overwhelming power of technology, and I am not saying that not only because of the introduction of the computer and the Internet and so on. It is the background to the technology that poses the threat. What I mean is the scientific mode of thought which is quite different to the way of thinking employed in the humanities. This scientific way of thinking penetrates widely, and profoundly — overwhelming all educational systems, and not only the school education systems, but also the media, the academic world and other areas. The minds of the people that once were forged by a humanities education now have been altered to espouse an analytic, exclusively scientific way of thinking. So literature and scientific technology are now not so intrinsically, logically compartmentalized.

Professor Hughes:

First of all, although there obviously are universal values like love, tolerance, truth and forgiveness and so on, I think that they are recognized universally is because they are to some extent very vague. That they are recognized universally is a crucial point, which is something that I will come back to in a moment. They are vague because each particular individual, let alone each particular culture, will give content to each of those values by building up a very large number of very small decisions, or sometimes large decisions, in the course of a life which explains exactly to them when truthfulness is important and why it is important and how it is important, as distinct from honesty, or tolerance or kindness or generosity. We only give content to these very general concepts in local circumstances. So I would like to distinguish between the shared but vague concepts and their local and highly particular applications.

There are good reasons why this should be true, for although we have a shared human nature, local parameters delimit what we can intelligibly say to one another. Human nature is extremely flexible and therefore we can give different content to most of those terms, while still communicating with one another, I don't think that it is possible to establish just one priority of values. It seems to me that there can be several equally legitimate priorities of values. People can stress the artistic, the intellectual, and the socially committed — various ways in which you can live a legitimate human life — reflecting different priorities of values and different cultures can do the same. Hence, I am convinced that the best method we have of reaching some kind of global togetherness is not by trying to look for a uniformity, but by sharing all the scientific knowledge that we have about human nature and its environment, sharing everything we know about medicine, ecology, but also about the effect of high-rise buildings on children and the effect of computers on education. If we shared that, then at least we know the limitations that human nature is putting upon us in different environments and therefore have an intelligent view of the choices that we must make.

I think that we have suffered by not having a sufficiently good scientific basis for ethics, and that if we are honest and looking for the truth, what we need is information, shared information, but we should not expect to come up with one set of shared answers, but a universally communicable set of different answers.

Professor Chou:

I would like to start with your point about whether there is basic or significant values in the arts. Obviously to me, the answer is "yes." It is especially so not only throughout Asian cultures, but the Chinese culture in particular. I want to say that the term *intellectual* in Chinese really means a person in the arts, and the word *arts* traditionally means both knowledge and creativity. So it is absolutely important that we pay attention to what knowledge represents in Asian societies and what creativity really is. So that takes us to the next question as whether an entire cultural heritage can be revitalized, certainly the answer can be "yes" — the question is how, and how depends on how we recognize the heritage of each society and through that recognition turn our attention to true creativity. Without revitalizing one's cultural heritage, there is no true creativity.

I also agree absolutely with your point regarding whether local and regional knowledge can be developed as universal. I have spent ten years in Yunnan dealing with minority peoples and their indigenous culture, and what one can learn from them is enormous, and this knowledge should be made known to other societies. In fact, as people involved in creativity in the twentieth century, we know that this is the true root of creativity throughout the world universally. So that, to me, is a very important point for us to recognize and it is obviously related to the question of cultural heritage. How to achieve cultural revitalization?

I would like to stress the role of education, from education to research, from research to creativity. Without research, meaning without knowledge, there is no creativity and no truth. You borrow other people's language, other people's ideas and other people's concepts, their original ideas. And you cannot have independent ideas unless you do research, but you cannot be qualified to do research unless you have education, so I want to bring you to my favourite point of view, namely, all that what we are discussing is far removed from reality unless we reform our education system. I think that I am in the wrong place to talk about this issue. I am the product of an Asian education, as well as American, and I know that for education in Asia, the more we reform our educational system, the less we know our own legacy. So I think the first point, the prerequisite is the emphasis on curriculum that deals with your own cultural heritage. That is the only way that one can be qualified to do research, gain knowledge and then to be creative. How can we do that? The first thing is to improve and reform education.

Professor King:

Chairman, I am not going to answer all the questions raised here. But are there universal values? To me, I think that because of the trend for globalization, humanity is faced with the very fundamental issue of surviv-ability and living conditions. It would be an unimaginable situation if you did not have a minimal level of values shared by different cultures. I believe that there is a minimum level of values shared by different peoples in the world, and it is simply a necessity to have that. So I would say that love, forgiveness — you use the word meta-language — that is certainly the precondition. Yes, I think that it is not necessarily to argue from an epistemological background of the conditions that are necessary for life.

Another point that I want to talk about is whether cultural legacies can be revitalized or not. I think the most important sense now that we are entering a new century is that we have forgotten so much about being Chinese. As a Chinese, when you talk about revitalization of a culture, its legacy, we must get to know its legacy again, and this can usually only be understood in the presence of context. This is why cultural legacy will be discovered again and again differently. So I think that at this moment, the cultural legacy for China or for Hong Kong can still be different. But to your question about whether we can go back to our roots, roots always have relevance to the present, so you go back to your roots and discover your present.

So what we should do for Hong Kong? I would say, like it or not, if you want to come a viable cultural entity, you must get back to your roots — this is the process of revitalization. But unfortunately, over the last one hundred years in China, all the cultural reform, all the so-called cultural revitalization involved trying to forget things. So what do you have? Now this is a very controversial point for me to make, that all the great brilliant intellectuals in the last fifty years, have all talked about re-evaluation of our culture, traditions and revitalization of the cultural legacy, but yet at the end of day, do away with it — as if by doing away with tradition, you become modern yourself. Now this is the question at the turn of the century, that we probably should reflect on more. Luckily, I think that globalization itself, as Tu Wei-ming pointed out, is also inevitably involved in the localization process, and it is not just the spread of Western modernity to other parts of the world. The process of globalization actually involves the discovering of local knowledge. So it inevitably has to play some role in the kind of cultural legacy being debated and discovered.

Professor Thévenot:

I think that what is lacking here is the question of criticism; because I think most of us here talk about globalization as if it were some sort of unique progressive path. So what we need a very strong instrument with which to critique this view. Of the many answers that have been given, a very strong one is the connection with local cultures and local knowledge. But I wonder whether we do not need some other view other than either a global or local one. Because this is always dangerous, since the global always seems to dominate the local. So global frequently means "the market" which is the most likely candidate to transcend boundaries of culture or boundaries of local knowledge. So we need to think of candidates other than the market or technical efficiency to be in a position to a build a positive critical framework and real critical pluralism.

Professor Kwok:

I think that the concept of critique is built-in in all these issues. We are criticizing and thinking critically, that is why critique as a concept as an issue has not been mentioned. And I think that the market and technology and all these things will be brought up during the course of this discussion.

Professor Nochlin:

I think that we have to be wary of believing that all cultures share even a vague sense of universal values. I mean, I don't think that is the case. I have just been reading a book about Nazi Germany, and they valued hardness, insensitivity, absoluteness, loyalty to party, etc. Those they thought were universal values and they tried to make other people agree with them. I think, I would like to believe that kindness, honesty, loyalty, kindness and courage, which are my values, are everybody's. But I am not sure that it is a failure of understanding, that there are cultures and groups that have generally very different values from mine and I think that values are often situational. You wouldn't want the same values to predominate in an army camp as in a nursery school. This is sort of utilitarian, that's obvious.

I also think should think of some of the minor virtues, which are I think are universal. Frivolity is a wonderful virtue that nobody has mentioned. And a little frivolity is a very good thing. Obsession — being obsessed, seems to me a wonderful and universal value. Nonchalance, too — I think they are virtues and we suffer when we don't include them.

I also think that, vis-à-vis tradition one has to be wary. There is a wonderful book by Eric Hobsbawm called *The Invention of Tradition* and he points out how often, in the very justifiable search for shared traditions, people come upon or actually invent certain practices and ways of doing things in the interest of local or national honour, or development which are really inventions more than discoveries. I think that every time you go back to tradition you are so right, you are reading it for your own time, you are recovering, reinventing it.

Finally, I would like to say in terms of implementation, I think that you need courage, I think that you need to work with other people — this is probably one of the things that is hard for intellectuals to do. But I think that one of the ways that gets things done is some sort of group organization and group activity, and I think being courageous and speaking out when necessary, refusing censorship, refusing to allow other people to be censored, especially for people with less power and less clout. But I think that one has to be an activist as well as an intellectual.

Professor Bowers:

I think one of the problems we are dealing with is the ability of modern technology to hide that we are moving beyond the ability of the earth's natural systems to revitalize themselves. The message is that of plenitude. You go to the market wherever you go and what seems deficient is the ability for our credit cards to handle what we are enticed into buying. I think that we are at a very critical point, and I would like to bring it up again that we have got to see what is not visible in the marketplace. What is not visible in the shopping malls.

That is, we are introducing 80,000 new chemicals into the environment pumping chemicals into the environment and don't have a clue of how many of these chemicals interact each other and how they effect our living systems. 40 percent of the arctic icecap has melted, not just displaced form one place to another, 40 percent of the icecap has melted since 1970. Many responsible institutions and individuals recognize global warming as phenomena, but many scientists indicate that we may be entering the sixth extinction and they point to the number of species that are rapidly declining. We are, at this time, narrowing the genetic basis of our food supply, and we are doing that radically. In India there is the possibility of 30,000 varieties of rice that are going to be displaced if Monsanto and other corporate aspects of agribusiness have their way in terms of introducing genetically altered super-rice varieties. I think that the question is what are the appropriate uses of technology and what is the inappropriate. And these questions become more complex, in terms of framing that discussion in terms of modern society, in terms of indigenous cultures with a strong sense of roots. The problem though is that universities are guardians and in fact determiners of what constitutes high status knowledge, and I would make the case that high status knowledge co-evolved with the industrial revolution so there is a double bind here. There have been very courageous groups who have challenged modernity. Donna Cheevers has said that science began as local science, as one of the local science and got universalized. These courageous groups included the Zapatistas of Chapas, the Chipco movement in India, and the indigenous cultures of the Andes where there was a flourishing of biological and agricultural knowledge.

Now the problem is that we don't see the cultural pattern that is reinforced by our different technologies. For the most part, academics share the same patterns that a taken-for-granted on a certain level and amplified by the technologies. It's a double bind. The only way we are going to democratize technology is by being able to clarify how it is different forms of technology alter our relationships, our patterns of thinking, and our sense of community and the kinds of skills that are vital to a non-hyper consumer-orientated lifestyle. So, I think, that there is an tremendous sense of responsibility that universities have to face up to, but I don't have a clue as how to reach colleagues who are educated to think in the patterns of the industrial revolution.

Professor Oliveros:

I am going to take a chance here and switch the modes that we are using, of using words, by switching everything and asking everyone to think about a sound, and the sound is "ahh." Is that sound good in Chinese? Can everybody understand "ahh"? I want to see if all of us in this room can do something together. This is a metaphor of how we can work together and support one another. I want to take this sound "ahh" and ask everyone to just sing together the sound "ahh." And I am not going to conduct this sound, I am just going to ask to begin and sound "ahh," sing "ahh" over several breathes so that we can feel everyone in the room come together on this particular sound. All the intellectuals who don't sing have to screw up their courage and just do it.

Now I have a very good Daoist teacher in the United States, a Chinese from Shanghai, his name is Master Xi. "Do you feel something?" He always asked when you did an exercise, "Do you feel something?" "Do you feel something?"

Professor Tu:

I'll try to respond to Marc Ferro's comment at the very beginning — it took me a while to register. I think that is linked to many of the questions raised. I want to suggest that an idea, a very useful concept in Chinese, but which has gained a lot of currency in lots of discussions, simply *ti zhi* 體知 that is translated as "embodied knowing" or "embodied knowledge." I think that his description is absolutely right, what happened in terms of actual existential circumstances in China is not just invasion or colonization from outside but explosion from within. Once you have just such a situation, the sense of it created a kind of void, a very powerful void, and we are maybe the first generation in that period, so now what is to be done? Some would say that there is nothing to be done. If you look at the Chinese Opium Wars to 1979, to use the Jewish experience of the Holocaust, numerous holocausts happened, millions of people died, yet its neighbours were not affected because China was in its self-imposed isolation, the region was not aware of it and the West was totally oblivious to it as well.

Since 1979, China, has by choice, and also by default, become an integral part of the global community in terms of ideas, formation, goods, services, migration — all kinds of things. So what happens to China? What are the consequences for the Asian-Pacific region, and perhaps for the rest of humanity? Now one commentator in the *Herald Tribune* made an observation, that for a civilization that was humiliated for so long frustrated for so long, there are only two powerful psychologies open to them—one is revenge and the other one is to settle scores. We have been victimized for so long, it's time for us to do something. To share power, perhaps to become a victimizer, that's the question I posed concerning what is the cultural message. If the cultural resources cannot be globalized or generalized to deal with the situation, the rules of the game, which are totally defined in terms of wealth and power, become internalised even among the very young. So you share the market, you are market sharing, and you try to enhance your power, and enhance your ability, while the less unfortunate will be even more marginalized. And we know that China now has maybe consumed or absorbed 40 percent, to 70 percent of investment. But anyway, the question I want to raise is this, what are some of the cultural resources if we take embodied knowledge as a point of departure? The assumption is that every human being is embedded into a particular situation, almost fated to be a particular person.

Now in many traditions, the assumption is have to take a position, an ideal view to the conditionally of your existence, you have to transcend your ethnicity, you engender all those things in order to be universal. And this has been the argument for some time. For now, is it possible for us to imagine a situation where all the conditionalities, constraints can be transformed into fruit for resources, for self-realization, and at the same time allowing all kinds of other people with their conditionalities as resources for self-preservation. I think the notion for that kind of self-realization is of a different kind of communication, it is not a communication of transcending one's position, it is a communication that is digging deeply into that particular situation and with an overview, in other words, there is, I think, the artistic representations — the sense of rage, the sense of indignation, the sense of anger, could be transformed into artistic expression of beauty and truth, that transformation is something that every person within a culture will have to be comfortable with.

If China begins to think that, the rules of defining the international community will have to be fundamentally changed. It is impossible for us in Hong Kong to imagine that India can serve as an important reference for our sense of human flourishing, just as Western Europe, or the United States, or Japan is at present. We will be a far wealthier power if we take India seriously. India, has a middle class of over 100 million, who speak English, they are very much are part of international culture more than we can ever become in the near future. India has experienced fifty years of democracy; this is something that people in China are still struggling to do. And India has always been a major exporting nation in terms of spiritual values. We could learn a great deal from them and broaden our reference points so that we may find values that are disvalues or unrelated to us become values. So I would say just one word about Ambrose King's points. It is not just how these values can become relevant to the modernizing process, but how we can become more critical of the modernizing process, without loosing sight of the positive aspect of it.

Notes on Contributors

C. A. Bowers

C. A. Bowers has taught at the University of Oregon and Portland State University, and is now semi-retired. He is a world renowned environmentalist and has been invited to speak all over the world. He gave the John Dewy Memorial Lecture in 1982, and is a member of the Jacques Ellul Society.

Professor Bowers has published twelve books and numerous articles. His most recent works include: *The Cultural Dimensions of Educational Computing: Understanding the Non-neutrality of Technology* (1988); (with David Flinders) *Responsive Teaching: An Ecological Approach to Classroom Patterns of Language, Culture, and Thought* (1990); *Education, Cultural Myths, and the Cultural Crisis: Toward Deep Changes* (1993); *Educating for an Ecologically Sustainable Culture: Rethinking Moral Education, Creativity, Intelligence, and Other Modern Orthodoxies* (1995); *The Culture of Denial: Why the Environmental Movement Needs a Strategy for Reforming Universities and Public Schools* (1997); *Let Them Eat Data* (2000); *Educating for Eco-Justice and Community* (2001).

Chan Sin-wai

Chan Sin-wai graduated from The Chinese University of Hong Kong and continued his studies at the School of Oriental and African Studies, University of London, where he received his Ph.D. degree. He is now Professor and Chairman of the Department of Translation, The Chinese University of Hong Kong. His teaching and research interests lie mainly in the areas of translation studies, machine translation and bilingual lexicography. His recent publications include *Translation in Hong Kong: Past, Present and Future* (The Chinese University Press, 2001) and *Longman Active Study English-Chinese Dictionary* (2001). He is also the Chief Editor of *Journal of Translation Studies*.

Chou Wen-chung

Although trained as a civil engineer in China, Chou Wen-chung turned to the study of music after going to the United States in 1946. There he studied with such composers as Otto Luening and Edgar Varèse. The relationship with Varèse was especially close, and following that composer's death, Chou completed his *Nocturnal*, a large-scale choral work. Within his own oeuvre, Chou has sought to bridge the gap between cultures by applying Asian aesthetic concepts to Western music. Chinese art and literature have provided the inspiration for many of his major compositions. Chou, who is currently Director of the Center for United States-China Arts Exchange, has also had enormous influence as professor of music at Columbia University.

Marc Ferro

Marc Ferro is president of the Association of Research at the Ecole des Hautes Etudes en Sciences Sociales and co-director of Annales, Economies, Societes, Civilisations. He is also former editorial secretary and member of the editorial committee of *Cahiers du Monde Russe et Sovietique*. He writes for anthologies and periodicals and his publications include: *The Great War 1914-1918* (1973); *The 1917 Revolution: A Social History of the Russian Revolution* (1980), *Cinema and History* (Contemporary Film Studies, 1988), *Nicholas II: Last of the Tsars* (1991), and *Colonization: A Global History* (1997).

Master Hsing Yun

Master Hsing Yun, the forty-eighth Patriarch of the Lin-chi (Japanese Rinzai) line of Ch'an, is the founder of the Fo Guang Shan Buddhist Order which has its international headquarters in Kaohsiung, Taiwan. He has set up over 171 branch temples around the world on five continents, and was the founder of 16 Buddhist colleges in Taiwan and Hsi Lai University in Los Angeles. He also founded Buddha's Light International Association (BLIA), having its Headquarters in L.A., U.S.A. in 1992. He is also an active philanthropist.

Master Hsing Yun set up the Tripitaka Editorial Committee which has already published *Agama Canon, Ch'an Canon, The Fo Guang Buddhist Dictionary,* and *The Buddhist Historical Chronology*. He has also founded two publishing houses: Fo Guang Publishing in Taiwan, and Hsi Lai

Publishing in the U.S. He was awarded an honorary Ph.D. by Oriental University, Los Angeles in 1978, and in 1984 was given an award by the Ministry of Education in Taiwan for his contribution to society. He has won numerous other awards and honours.

Gerard Hughes

After degrees in Philosophy, Classics and Theology, Professor Hughes undertook doctoral studies in ethics at the University of Michigan. He has been active in university administration as head of the Department of Philosophy, vice-principal of Heythrop College, London University, member of the University of London's Academic Council and is presently master of Campion Hall, Oxford. He has twice been Austin Fagothey Visiting Professor at the University of Santa Clara, California. His publications include *Authority in Morals* (Chapman and Georgetown University Press, 1978), *Moral Decisions* (Darton, Longman and Todd, 1980), *The Philosophical Assessment of Theology* (1987), *The Nature of God* (1995) in the series *The Problems of Philosophy* (Routledge) and *Aristotle on Ethics* (Routledge, 2001). He has also written several academic articles for *The New Dictionary of Christian Ethics* edited by J. Macquarrie and J. Childress, and selected the readings on twentieth century moral philosophy and the philosophy of religion for *A Dictionary of Philosophical Quotations* edited by A. J. Ayer and J. O'Grady (Blackwell).

Paul Kan Man-lok

Paul Kan Man-lok, a graduate of The Chinese University of Hong Kong, is chairman of Champion Technology Holdings Limited and Kantone Holdings Limited, which are both listed on the Hong Kong Stock Exchange. He is also chairman of Multitone Electronics PLC and Multiton Electonik.

Mr. Kan has been in the telecommunications and computing industry for thirty years, and is best known for the development of the world-first multilingual pager (the Kantone Pager) in 1987. Mr. Kan was awarded the First Electronic Design Competition Award in 1988; the Governor's Award for Industry in 1989; the 1992 Young Industrialist Award and the Enterprise Trophy of the 1993 Hong Kong Business Awards; and in Europe, the 1994 International Trophy for Technology and Quality. In China, Mr. Kan was invited to become advisor and vice-president of the executive committee of the Chinese Literature Foundation; the honorary president of the Telemetry and Telecontrol Research Institute of the Ministry of Information Industry; and a member of the Chinese People's Political Consultative Conference of Anhui Province.

Shuichi Kato

Literary critic, author and physician, Shuichi Kato was born in Tokyo in 1919. He graduated from the Medical School of Tokyo University in 1943, and received an M.D. from the same university in 1950, specializing in hematology. Professor Kato has had a distinguished career as a critic and commentator on Japanese culture, literature and arts. He is a noted literary figure in his own right; and has contributed to deepening understanding of Japanese culture worldwide through his teaching and writing. In recognition of his outstanding achievements, he has received the order of Officer des Arts et des Lettres from the French government in March 1993 for his history of Japanese Literature, *Nihon bunkagaku shi josetsu* (1975), and in Japan he has received the prestigious Asahi Prize in January 1994 for his contribution to post-war Japanese culture.

He is internationally known for his books on Japanese art, society and literature, which have been published in several languages including Chinese, Italian, German, French and English. His most important works in English include *Form, Style, Tradition: Reflections on Japanese Art and Society* (1971), the three volume *A History of Japanese Literature* (1979), and *Japan: Spirit and Form.*

Ambrose Y. C. King

Ambrose Yeo-chi King is Acting Vice-Chancellor and Chair Professor of sociology at The Chinese University of Hong Kong. He has been Visiting Fellow at the Center of International Studies, MIT (1976) and the University of Heidelberg (1985). He was elected Fellow (academician), Academia Sinica (1994). His publications include a number of books and numerous articles on development and modernization of Chinese societies. He has been editorial board member of journals including *The Journal of Applied Behavioral Science* and *The China Quarterly.* He has held many advisory positions to the Hong Kong Government such as the Independent Commission Against Corruption (ICAC), the Law Reform Commission, the University Grants Committee's Research Grant Council. He was appointed non-official Justice of the Peace in 1994, and was awarded the

Silver Bauhinia Star of the Hong Kong Special Administrative Region and Doctor of Literature, *Honoris Causa* of the Hong Kong University of Science and Technology in 1998.

Kwok Siu Tong

Kwok Siu Tong, Dean of the Faculty of Arts (1998–2001), graduated from The Chinese University of Hong Kong in 1972 and obtained his master and doctoral degrees from the University of California at Berkeley. His training is in comparative and cross-cultural studies of modern Chinese and European history.

He has taught at the Department of History, The Chinese University of Hong Kong since 1977, and published more than eleven books and over sixty articles. He is an advisor to a number of universities in China, including Tsinghua University and Foreign Affairs College. He is a Visiting Professor of the Faculty of Arts, Fudan University and Sichuan University, and Special Research Fellow of the Department of History, Peking University.

Linda Nochlin

Linda Nochlin was born in 1931 in New York. She holds a B.A. from Vassar College (1951), and an M.A. from Columbia University (1952) and a Ph.D. from New York University. She is the Lila Acheson Wallace Professor of Modern Art of the Institute of Fine Arts, New York University. She specializes in the art of the nineteenth and twentieth centuries, with a particular interest in the work of Gustave Courbet and the impressionists. Before joining the faculty at New York University's Institute of Fine Arts, Professor Nochlin taught at Vassar, the Graduate Center of the City University of New York, and Yale University. She held fellowships at the American Academy of Arts and Sciences, the Institute for the Humanities, and the Institute for Advanced Study. She was also the 1997 New York Council for the Humanities Scholar. Linda Nochlin's recent publications include: *Representing Women* (1999), *Realism* (1997), *Andy Wahol: Nudes* (co-author, 1997); *The First 38 Years* (co-author, 1997); *Women in the 19ᵗʰ Century: Categories and Contradictions* (1997); *Renoir's Portraits: Impressions of an Age* (co-author, 1997), *The Jew in the Text* (1995) and *Florine Stettheimer: Manhattan Fantastica* (1995).

Pauline Oliveros

For decades Pauline Oliveros has explored the boundaries between performance and composition through improvisation, electronic sound production, theatre, ritual and meditation. She has collaborated extensively with dancers and other artists in the creation of mixed-media performances. Her aesthetic ideals are expressed in her publications, especially *Software for People: Collected Writings, 1963-1980.* Pauline Oliveros taught electronic music at the University of California at San Diego for fourteen years and influenced many musicians during her teaching career. In addition, she has served in an advisory capacity for organizations such as The National Endowment for the Humanities and the New York State Council for the Arts. Her compositions have earned her several awards including the Pacifica Foundation National Prize (U.S.), the Gaudeamus Prize (Netherlands) and the Beethoven Prize (Germany).

Isaac Stern

Isaac Stern was born in 1920. He made his public debut at the age of eleven in San Francisco. Following his studies at the San Francisco Conservatory, Stern actively pursued a performance career in the United States and after World War II, in Europe. The film *From Mao to Mozart: Isaac Stern in China* recorded his commitment to using music as a means of cross-cultural communication. He has recorded extensively as both a chamber musician and as a soloist. Aside from his role as performer, Stern has made major contributions to world musical culture through his efforts to develop new as well as existing arts institutions. In the U.S. he was deeply involved in saving Carnegie Hall from destruction and was instrumental in establishing The National Endowment for the Arts. He also helped to advance the careers of many younger musicians through his work with the America-Israel Cultural Foundation.

Laurent Thévenot

Laurent Thévenot is a professor at the Ecole des Hautes Etudes en Sciences Sociales (Paris) and Senior Researcher at the Centre d'Etudes de l'Emploi. Currently director of the Groupe de Sociologie Politique et Morale (EHESS-CNRS), he co-authored, with Luc Boltanski, *De la Jusification.* This book, which analyses the most legitimate forms of evaluation governing political, economic and social relationships, has been influential in new

French institutional economics and sociology. Other publications in the so-called "economie des conventions" include *Conventions Economies* and *Le Travail: Marches, Règles, Conventions* (this last book was co-edited with Robert Salais). He recently edited two books on new approaches of action, the practical engagement of objects and social cognition: *Les Objets dans l'action* (with Bernard Conein and Nicolas Dodier); *Cognition et information en societé* (with Bernard Conein). A book co-edited with Michel Lamont, *Comparing Cultures and Polities: Repertoires of Evaluation in France and the United States* has recently been published by Cambridge University Press.

Tu Wei-ming

Tu Wei-ming was born in Kunming, China and educated in Taiwan (B.A. at Tunghai University) and the U.S.A. (M.A. and Ph.D. at Harvard University). Before joining Harvard University as professor of Chinese History and Philosophy in 1981, Professor Tu taught Chinese intellectual history at Princeton University and the University of California at Berkeley. He has also lectured on Confucian humanism at Peking University, Taiwan National University, The Chinese University of Hong Kong, and the University of Paris. He is the author of: *Neo Confucian Thought*; *Wang Yang-ming's Youth Centrality and Commonality*; *Humanity and Self-cultivation*; *Confucian Thought: Selfhood as Creative Transformation* and *Way, Learning and Politics: Essays on the Confucian Intellectual*.

A member of the Committee on the Study of Religion at Harvard, the chair of the Academica Sinica's advisory committee on the Institute of Chinese Literature and Philosophy, and a fellow of the American Academy of Arts and Sciences, Tu Wei-ming is currently interpreting Confucian ethics as a spiritual resource for the emerging global community. He assumed his tenure as director of the Harvard-Yenching Institute in January 1996.

Wang Meng

Born in Beijing in 1934, Wang Meng was formerly minister of culture of the People's Republic of China from 1987 to 1990 and is currently a writer, research fellow and member of the National Standing Committee of the Chinese People's Political Consultative Conference.

Wang Meng has published over sixty books since 1955, including six novels, ten short story collections, as well as other works of poetry, prose and critical essays. His works have been translated and published in twenty-one different languages. He was made a member of the International Writing Program at the University of Iowa in 1980, was guest of honour of the Forty-eighth Congress of International Pen, New York in 1986, visiting scholar at Harvard University in 1993, and presidential fellow at Trinity College, Connecticut in 1998.

Index